# THE
# STAMP-PAD
# PRINTING
# BOOK

# THE STAMP-PAD PRINTING BOOK

## Florence H. Pettit

*Illustrated with designs and drawings by the author*

*and with photographs by*

Robert M. Pettit

THOMAS Y. CROWELL    NEW YORK

## To Fatfingers

Copyright © 1979 by Florence H. Pettit
All rights reserved. Printed in the United States of America.
No part of this book may be used or reproduced in any manner
whatsoever without written permission except in the case of
brief quotations embodied in critical articles and reviews.
For information address Thomas Y. Crowell, 10 East 53rd Street,
New York, N.Y. 10022. Published simultaneously in Canada by
Fitzhenry & Whiteside Limited, Toronto.
Designed by Harriett Barton

*Library of Congress Cataloging in Publication Data*

Pettit, Florence Harvey.
The stamp-pad printing book.
Includes index.
SUMMARY: Directions for using a stamp pad and paper
to print bookmarks, notepaper, posters, greeting cards,
wrapping paper, and many other useful things.
1. Rubber stamp printing—Juvenile literature.
[1. Rubber stamp printing. 2. Handicraft] I. Title.
TT867.P47 1979    761    78-22504
ISBN 0-690-03967-0    ISBN 0-690-03968-9 lib. bdg.

10   9   8   7   6   5   4   3   2   1

FIRST EDITION

# CONTENTS

# 1. A KNIFE,
# AN ERASER, A STAMP
# PAD, AND PAPER
## *Basic Tools and Materials*

Stamp-pad printing is a modern-day version of a craft that is thousands of years old. Throughout the world many different kinds of blocks and stamps have been used to print on a variety of materials. Designs and symbols were modeled in clay and carved on bone, leather, and wood. Pigments were applied to these primitive blocks, and patterns were stamped on animal hides, papyrus, and cloth. Eventually, printing of one sort or another came into use in every corner of the earth.

In stamp-pad printing, instead of carving your design on a wooden block, or on bone, your stamps will be cut by hand on ordinary erasers, and your pigments will be bright-colored inks from office stamp pads. You can carve letters, or use a ready-made alphabet set for your printing, too. With only a few designs and letters you can stamp greeting cards, gift-wrapping papers, and decorative papers to cover boxes and notebooks. You can print signs, posters, and cloth banners, and use your own ideas to make all kinds of things.

To begin to print with stamps, you need very few tools and materials, all of which are available in toy and hobby shops, art stores, or wherever school and office supplies are sold. You may already have some of them. Here are the principal things you will need:

BASIC TOOLS AND MATERIALS

Small X-Acto knife
Eraser to carve
Stamp pad
Paper on which to print
Pocketknife
Ruler
Piece of transparent tracing paper
Sheet of clear acetate plastic

_____

And later you may want to buy an inexpensive ready-made printing set of alphabet letters.

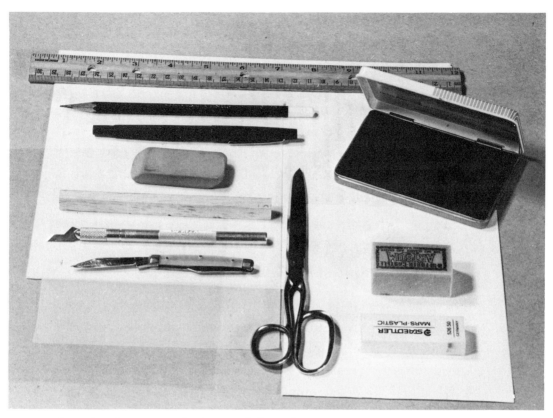

*Materials for stamp pad printing, clockwise from the ruler: stamp pad, artgum eraser, white eraser, scissors, pocketknife, X-Acto knife, wooden guide stick, pink eraser, felt-tip pen, pencil; and scratch paper, vellum paper, and a sheet of clear acetate plastic.*

In using these simple tools and materials, you will soon discover for yourself some of the reasons for the enjoyment that has always been a part of hand printing.

*The Principal Tool*

The actual-size drawing shows the X-Acto knife used to carve the eraser stamps. You can buy the knife handle and a small packet of No. 16 blades to fit it at art and hobby stores everywhere for less than two dollars. In carving, the knife is held like a pencil. If you can write, you can certainly carve an eraser!

*Some Things to Know About Erasers*

There are two kinds of erasers that are best to use: artgum, which can be found almost everywhere in school-supply and art stores; and white plastic or soap erasers, which are sold mostly in art stores.

The first kind—artgum—is made by Faber-Castell and comes in three sizes: small, $\frac{7}{8}$ by 1 by 1 inch; medium, $\frac{7}{8}$ by 1 by 2 inches; and large, $1\frac{1}{16}$ by $1\frac{3}{4}$ by $2\frac{3}{16}$ inches. A single artgum eraser can be sliced up to make two or three small stamps about $\frac{1}{2}$ inch thick. After you have carved and stamped your first design in artgum, you will discover that the tiny bubbles throughout this rather soft tan eraser will leave small white spots in your finished prints. This characteristic of artgum, and the fact that it is also a bit crumbly, mean that the eraser is apt to break if you use it for cutting small, detailed designs and letters. Artgum is fine, however, for simple designs, and you probably won't mind the small white flecks in your prints. Artgum was used to stamp quite a few of the designs in this book, and it prints a good impression when used for bold designs and big, square letters.

Two or more artgums can be stuck together with rubber cement to make a stamp for a larger design. To do this, first coat the sides or ends that are to be joined with rubber cement, using the brush that comes in the small jar or can of cement. Allow the cement on both surfaces to dry. It is very important to keep the two surfaces you plan to carve perfectly flat, with no bump at the joint. The best way to do this is to hold the erasers, one in each hand, with the sides that are to

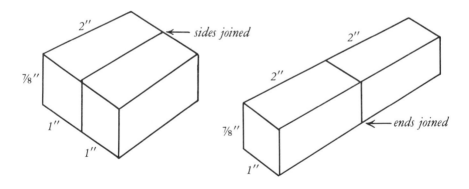

be carved *facedown*, flat on your worktable, and the two cement-coated sides or ends facing each other. Now, keeping both erasers in line, flat on the table, move them toward each other and press them together. They will "join" immediately. Since two erasers are seldom exactly the same size, the two uppermost sides may not meet to make a perfectly flat surface: the bottom side is the one that should be used for carving.

Sometimes a white hairline can be seen in a print where erasers have been cemented together, but usually this is not pronounced enough to spoil the design. Certain stamps can be planned so that no printing surface will occur where there is a seam. Both the clown head and the Santa Claus, shown below, were printed from stamps made by sticking two artgums together.

If you want to carve an artgum eraser that appears to have a whitish or slightly shiny surface, you must first dull the surface. To do this, hold the eraser, firmly placed against a sheet of paper, flat on the table, and rub it back and forth and

in a circle several times. When you transfer a design to the rubbed surface, your pencil lines will show up far better. If you want to mark and carve the surface of an eraser where the manufacturer's name has been printed, rub the lettering off with a pencil eraser.

The second type of eraser, the white plastic or soap eraser, is available in several varieties. One kind, the German-made white Staedtler Mars eraser, is excellent for carving and printing. It comes in three sizes: small, $\frac{1}{2}$ by $\frac{3}{4}$ by $1\frac{5}{8}$ inches; medium, $\frac{1}{2}$ by $\frac{7}{8}$ by $2\frac{1}{2}$ inches; and large—labeled Grand—$\frac{9}{16}$ by $1\frac{1}{2}$ by 3 inches. The largest size is the best buy, but sometimes the 3-inch edges of this eraser are slightly rounded. Two strips about $\frac{1}{16}$ inch wide must then be cut off the edges of the printing sides in order to make a completely flat surface. Thus the printing area is really $1\frac{3}{8}$ inches wide instead of $1\frac{1}{2}$ inches.

Another kind of white eraser is made by Faber-Castell and is called Magic Rub. It measures $\frac{1}{2}$ by 1 by $2\frac{3}{16}$ inches. It is more rubbery and a little less easy to carve than the Mars brand, but it is OK. Some printers use an eraser called Rub-kleen made by Eberhard-Faber and find it satisfactory. There is still another white eraser called Vinyl, which is not recommended because the rubber is tough and hard to carve.

All the white erasers cost a little more than artgum, but they generally have a fine, even consistency that cuts as easily as cheese, and they print a solid, even impression on paper, cloth, or wood. White erasers do not crumble; they almost never break; and they can be used for bold as well as for very detailed designs.

Using fast-drying epoxy glue, two white erasers can be stuck together to accommodate a larger design. Follow the directions on the two tubes, spreading the glue thinly on both erasers with the tab on the tube. Press them together while holding them flat on the table, in the same way that has already been prescribed for joining two artgum erasers. Epoxy glue does not bond instantly like rubber cement, so leave the erasers in place for at least five minutes, and preferably longer, while the glue dries. The black printing on white erasers can be removed by rubbing it hard with extra-fine steel wool, or by rubbing it with nail-polish remover.

On the whole, white erasers are better than artgums for making carved rubber stamps and are worth the few extra cents they cost. You can judge for yourself the way the two kinds of erasers work by trying them both out.

There are other types of erasers, but they are unsuited to carving. Pink, red, and gray erasers are fine for erasing pencil marks, but they are too tough and rubbery to be carved. Gray kneaded erasers are too soft to be made into stamps. The Mars white erasers are not only the easiest to carve and best for printing, but you can also erase pencil guidelines with them without leaving a trace, so save a small scrap for *erasing.*

*Some Things to Know About Stamp Pads*

Good, generally available stamp pads are the *felt* pads (not sponge) made by Carter. They come in small, flat tin boxes in one of three sizes. No. 0 is $2\frac{1}{4}$ by $3\frac{1}{2}$ inches; No. 1 is 2 $\frac{3}{4}$ by $4\frac{1}{8}$ inches and is the best size for your stamp-pad printing. The large No. 2 pad, measuring 3 by 6 inches, is needed only for whatever large stamps you may make by gluing erasers together. Office-supply stores and stationers sell inked stamp pads and the two-ounce bottles of Carter's ink used to renew them. The stamp pads and inks come in red, blue, green, purple—nice lively colors—and black. Take good care of your stamp pads. When they are not in use, keep the lids of the boxes closed. If the cloth covering over the felt pad dries out a little, or if you have used up so much ink that the color begins to look pale, follow the very simple directions on the goose-necked plastic bottle to reink the pad.

Should crumbs or scraps of rubber from a newly cut stamp be deposited on your ink pad, blow or scrape the bits off gently with the blade of a pocketknife. Such scraps will definitely interfere with the inking. Be careful also never to press a stamp that already has one color of ink on it against a pad of a different color. There is no way to remove the wrong color from the pad, and that spot will always be spoiled. It's difficult to work with a pad that has such a place. You need the whole surface to get good, even inking on your stamps.

*Some Things to Know About Paper*

The kind of paper you use is important, for it has a lot to do with how your final print will look. Any ordinary, rather hard-surfaced, smooth white paper, such as typewriter paper, takes stamp-pad impressions very well. Most stationery, post-cards, plain notebook sheets, smooth drawing paper, and Kraft wrapping paper also work well.

Three kinds of paper that are not so good to use are slick or shiny papers, which are nonabsorbent and on which prints will look blotchy; rough-textured or linen-like papers, on which prints will show the texture and colors will be grayed; and very soft, absorbent papers, such as newspaper and cheap construction paper, which act as blotters and allow ink to spread and blur.

Colored paper often adds to the gay appearance of greeting cards and other stamp-pad projects. The black-and-white photographs of printed cards, and so on, that appear throughout this book cannot show you how colorful the objects really are. Papers in pale clear colors and light soft hues are good for printing, but dark or intense colors like red, brown, and purple will affect the color of the impression. On very dark paper, the printing cannot be seen at all. Stamp-pad ink is transparent—except for black—so that the color of the paper will always show through the ink a little. Blue ink, for instance, will look greenish on a deep yellow paper, because blue and yellow together make green. Experiment with colored papers after you have made a proof on white. If white seems to give the best results, then use it; colors usually look their cleanest on white paper. You can print on white paper and mount the print on a larger piece of bright-colored paper to get a more vivid effect.

One last word about paper. The better the quality of the paper, the better the appearance of the finished work. Good papers have a look and feel to them that will enhance your printing and make the time spent on carving and printing your designs seem very much worth while.

# 2. CARVING
# AND PRINTING
## *Three Practice Designs*

All the decorative designs in this book (except for the small cartoons and animals that come with some ready-made lettering sets) were printed from carvings made on erasers. The best way to learn the craft is to start off with very simple designs. Then, when you have had some practice and know how to trace a drawing, transfer it to an eraser, and carve and print from it, you will be able to make any sort of decorative stamp you want. Your own original designs and pictures can be made and printed in the same way.

The three designs shown on page 13 are good ones to begin with. The drawings are planned to fit on the end of a medium-size (⅞ by 1 by 2 inches) artgum eraser. All are straight-line designs that are easy to cut. Also shown are the finished prints made from the stamps.

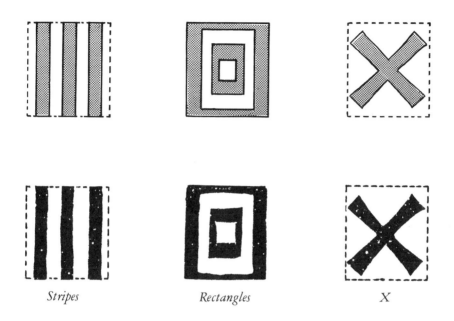

Stripes          Rectangles          X

To make the stamps and print them, you will need a medium-size artgum eraser, an X-Acto knife with blade, a No. 1 inked felt stamp pad (why not start with the color red?), a 9- by 12-inch sheet of transparent tracing paper, a piece of clear acetate plastic about 6 by 8 inches—like a notebook-sheet protector—a soft pencil, a ruler, a ball-point pen, and some plain white paper to use for printing practice. Borrow from your household: transparent tape, a penknife or pocket-knife, a sharp butcher knife, and a wooden cutting board.

*Carving Designs*

Start by dividing the length of the artgum—2 inches—into three equal sections. Use the ruler and the ball-point pen to measure and mark off two lines straight across the eraser. Extend the lines down one side of the eraser. Put the eraser on the cutting board, and with the butcher knife make straight-down cuts exactly on the lines. Do not saw the knife back and forth and do not rock it—just press straight down on the handle of the knife and the back of the blade. This will give you three stamps on which to carve the practice designs. And the three little stamps are thick enough to hold easily for printing. Of course you can carve on any of the six surfaces of a stamp, but if you want to carve on two sides of the same eraser, use two opposite sides, not two adjoining sides, because the cutaway edges of one surface will also be cut away on the side next to it.

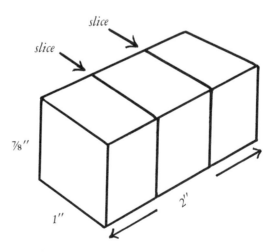

To trace the first diagram—the Stripes—put the sheet of clear plastic over the book page (to protect the page from pencil indentations) and with tape fasten a 2-inch square of tracing paper to the plastic. With a soft pencil, trace the design, following the outlines of the three straight bars and also the dotted outlines at the edges. Use the ruler to help you trace the straight lines.

Remove the tracing from the plastic and put it facedown (penciled side down) on the eraser, so that the outlines match the edges of the artgum. Bend down two opposite sides of the paper and hold them tight against the sides of the eraser. With the first finger or thumbnail of your other hand, rub or scratch firmly over the traced lines, or rub them with the back of the pocketknife blade. This will transfer the tracing to the eraser. There are two reasons for using *transparent* tracing paper: it allows you to see the lines of the drawing you want to trace, and also to see from the back where the traced lines are, so you can rub them to make the transfer. If the lines of your transfer are not clearly visible on the eraser, redraw them with a sharp soft pencil.

There is an important point to remember when planning designs to be carved for printing. It is the cutaway parts of the eraser surface that *will not print.* All of the surface that is left standing will receive the ink from the stamp pad and *will therefore print.* Before you start carving, it is a good idea to shade in lightly with pencil the areas you intend to leave standing—the shading will help to guide you in cutting the stamp. (The parts to be left uncut—or standing—in the practice designs are lightly shaded on the diagram.)

*A special note:* Any design, whether pencil tracing or drawing, that is to be transferred to the surface of an eraser must always be *reversed;* that is, placed facedown on the side you are to carve. Or, if you want to draw the design directly on the eraser, it must be drawn backward in order for it to print right side up. In a design as simple as the Stripes, this will not seem to matter at all, but in lettering or for a design that, when printed, must face in a certain direction, your carving *must* be in reverse. Many a beginner has carefully cut his or her initials on a stamp or block, only to discover that the letters were backward when printed!

Use the pen to number the four sides of your stamp. The stripes or bars should run from side 1 to side 3, as shown in the drawing. Now you are ready to start carving.

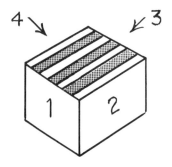

The goal is to cut away the unwanted, nonprinting part of the eraser surface with as few cuts as possible. This will produce a clear-cut design, as you can see in the photograph of the completed stamps. You should not hack away or chew at a design with the X-Acto knife when you carve. In the design for the Stripes, you simply want to cut away the nonprinting areas of the surface along two edges and between the three bars. Slanting cuts made at the same depth will remove the unwanted wedge-shaped strips between the bars. Each single slanted cut should meet another slanted cut made from the opposite direction. This may sound confusing, but if you follow the order of the cuts you are to make as described on the next page, the method will soon become clear to you.

*Four finished stamps—the Stripes, the X, the Rectangles, and a heart from Chapter 3.*

To cut, hold the knife as you would hold a pencil, but with the top of the knife tilted a little toward the back of your hand. This tilt of the knife is the secret of carving so that your prints will always be sharp. Do not hold the knife straight up and down, and do not cut straight down on the drawn lines. All cuts should slant a little. This will give the printing areas slanted sides and a strong wide base to stand on. The drawings show an end view of two stamps, one well cut, one poorly cut.

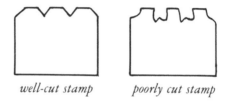

well-cut stamp          poorly cut stamp

When cutting, hold the eraser on the table with one hand and hold the knife in the other hand. Keep your fingers well away from the direction of your knife cuts. To make the first cut, start with side 1 of the eraser facing you, and pull the knife toward you along the first line, the one at the far left. A continuous slanted cut will remove one edge of the stamp. Give the stamp a half-turn so that side 3 faces you. Make the second cut as shown in the drawing, straight down the length of the other side of the same bar, pulling the knife toward you exactly as before. Turn the stamp again and make a third

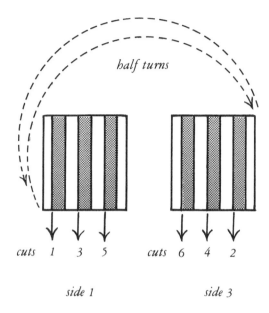

half turns

cuts  1  3  5        cuts  6  4  2

side 1                    side 3

slanted cut in the opposite direction, to meet the second cut; remove the cut strip from the groove.

The reason you should turn the stamp for each new cut in this design is to allow you to see the guidelines. You will always be cutting *to the left* of the area that is to remain standing. This is the logical way for a right-handed person to cut. Of course, if you are left-handed, you should reverse the procedure.

Keep turning the stamp in half-turns after each straight cut, following the order shown in the drawing. The last cut—6—will remove the other edge of the stamp.

The drawings show the angle at which to tilt the knife in order to groove out the nonprinting areas. The end view of side 1 shows the angle at which you hold the knife for cuts 1, 3, and 5. The end view of side 3 shows the *same* angle for cuts 2, 4, and 6, but for this you pull the knife in the opposite direction from cuts 1, 3, and 5.

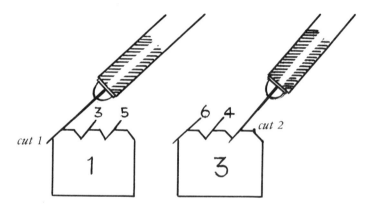

The two slanted sides of the little grooves you are cutting away should be cut sharply and smoothly, always at the same depth, in one continuous stroke so that the two cuts meet at the bottom of the groove. The wedge-shaped strips should come out cleanly. Do not pull at a partly cut piece of eraser

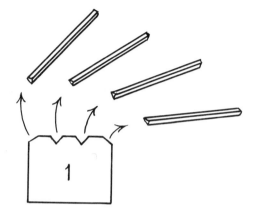

to try to remove it. Artgum breaks off easily, and you may accidentally tear off some areas you wanted to leave standing and spoil your stamp. If necessary, go over the cuts again until they are deep enough to meet at the base of the groove; then the strips will come out easily.

This grooving method for removing unwanted areas of an eraser is the principal method used to get rid of nonprinting surface on all stamps. When you have finished cutting, rub off or blow off any crumbs of artgum that may have been left on your stamp.

As you can see by looking at one end of your own stamp,

the slanting sides of the groove have left the printing areas standing on a wide base that is very firm and not apt to break. A poorly cut stamp—one with straight-sided cuts, or with cuts that go in *under* a printing area—will be likely to suffer damage in printing or cleaning.

If your first practice stamp is not as sharp and accurate as you want it to be, simply turn the eraser over and try again. You can decide afterward which of the two carved surfaces you want to keep, and with the butcher knife, slice off the more imperfect side. This will give the back of the stamp a flat surface against which to place your fingers so that you can achieve even pressure when you are printing. But before you can really judge the cutting, you need to see a print of your stamp. Some printers ink and print the trial proof of a stamp even before the carving is finished; this is a good way to check the progress of the cutting as you go along.

### Printing

When you make your first print, you will discover that this is by far the easiest and quickest part of the craft. Here is where the fun really begins.

To make a proof of your stamp, it is best to use plain white paper (a new sheet or the back of a discarded letter, etc.), because you can see your printing most clearly on white. Press the carved eraser firmly on the pad once or twice to ink the stamp. Then press the inked stamp firmly down on the paper and *do not move it* once you have placed it on the paper. Now lift the stamp and examine the print and also the stamp itself to see if there are any dabs of ink where the surface has not been cut deeply enough away. This is unlikely to happen with this particular design, but it may with others where there is more open background. If you see bits of ink on the stamp, do corrective cutting to remove them. When using the knife, cut away from the design, not toward it, whenever possible.

When you have printed a final satisfactory proof, be sure to clean the stamp. This is simple to do: on a piece of scratch paper, "stamp off" the remaining ink by making a row of ever-fading impressions until no more ink can be seen on the paper. Cleaning the ink off a stamp is a nuisance, but it must be done. Any ink left on a stamp will darken or otherwise change the impression printed from the next color used, even after several days have passed. Black ink seems to be the most persistent and damaging to subsequent bright, clear ink colors. So take time to stamp off all traces of ink, especially black, after each printing session. For a final cleaning before putting the stamp away, rub it gently and lightly with a very soft dry cloth. Do not rub *across* any delicately cut parts of the design.

*Two More Stamps*

Now try your hand at making the second practice stamp—the Rectangles. It requires some slightly different kinds of cutting, but it is only a little more complicated than the striped design. In this case, the eraser's edges are left standing to form the outer borders of the stamp, and instead of taking out narrow strips, your cutting will remove one hollow rectangle and one small square. Look at the photograph of the stamp on page 17.

The cuts must be slanted as before, and this time you must be careful not to cut past or into the corners of the areas that are to be left standing (as shaded on the drawing). Figure out the direction of your cuts so that the area that must remain to print is always to the right of your knife, and the knife is to the left of the line you are cutting. As before, always cut toward yourself. In this case, you can probably remove the area around the smaller rectangle with a total of eight cuts—two adjoining cuts along each side. Turn the stamp when the direction of a line changes. Begin in the upper right-hand corner of the design, and proceed from there.

Incidentally, if you find another way of carving an eraser that works better for you than the method described here, by all means use it. This method is not the only way of carving.

If you go on now to cut the third practice design, the big

X, it will add to your experience so that soon you will be expert enough to do almost any cutting. A cross is a traditional design that is also decorative, and the stamp will be useful for several projects.

Start cutting around the outline of the X with slanting cuts, keeping the knife to the left of the lines and turning the stamp as necessary between cuts. As before, make continuous cuts, following each line of the design until it changes direction. It is difficult to remove the knife and put it back into the eraser without making a break in the line. In fact, sometimes if the knife is removed, you can't even see where the first part of a cut was!

When the X is completely outlined with the first slanting cuts, go back in the opposite direction and make another set of slanting cuts to join those of the outline cuts. Remove the thin triangular-shaped pieces from the grooves. There is more nonprinting area in this design than there was in the first two. Do not try to cut it out by gouging, by chopping away, or by cutting straight in under the surface to remove these areas of eraser. A better and safer way, one that will not damage the cross, is to continue making small adjoining grooves in the open areas until you are safely away from the lines. Keep cutting the grooves more deeply until they are at least $\frac{1}{8}$ inch below the surface of the big X itself. Your first proof

will show you where you may have to cut still more deeply.

At the corners of the stamp and along the edges, between the arms of the cross, you can use the pocketknife to shave away very carefully these open areas, so they will not pick up ink from the stamp pad.

In very small areas it is impossible to use the pocketknife, and all small details and outlines should be cut by making grooves with the X-Acto knife. The stamps for the holly design and the cat show this clearly.

In all designs, the more open the area, the more deeply it must be cut. Very close to the cross, or to any unit that is part of the print, the background need not be cut away so deeply. Experience will show you how this works. Once the design is outlined with a groove, direct your cuts *away* from it whenever you can. Make trial proofs and clear away the background until the design prints sharply and is well defined.

Clean the stamp.

By now you may have noticed that no matter how precise and geometric a design or drawing is, the print made from the finished stamp looks less precise: the print has a hand-blocked look that is not apparent in the drawing. Every carver's stamp will be a little different from one cut by another person who traced and cut the same design. In the nineteenth century, when wood blocks were used to print cloth, the "block cut-

*A rubbing from an eighteenth century wood block owned by the Rhode Island Historical Society.*

ter" was the highest-paid person in the printworks. To this day, some experts can recognize fabrics printed by certain famous French and English woodblock cutters and engravers. And you may be sure that the work of the best carver looked slightly different from the drawing he had transferred to his block or plate.

Care and precision in cutting give hand block printing its strong, incisive appearance, but it is the little variations that occur in carving the stamp that make each printer's work distinctive.

# 3. MAKING
# A VALENTINE

A valentine heart is a perfect shape on which to learn about carving a rounded form, since a heart is *all* curves! A quick look at the valentines in this chapter will show you a few of the many ways there are to use only two elements—the heart stamp and your own handwritten message—to make a good-looking greeting.

You will need the eight basic articles listed in Chapter 1, plus scissors and a fine-pointed red felt pen. Of course, your stamp pad should be red. The drawing of the heart shown on page 31 is the right size to fit on the end of a $\frac{7}{8}$- by 1-inch artgum. For carving it, you can use a slice from a 2-inch eraser.

In the same way as in Chapter 2, put the sheet of plastic over the drawing of the heart and use tracing paper and a soft pencil to trace the design and the outlines around it. Transfer the drawing to the eraser in reverse, and redraw the lines in pencil if necessary.

Before you start carving, you must decide how you want the heart to look. Do you want a red heart to print on white paper, or a white heart in a red square? To make a solid red heart, you leave the heart standing and cut away the area around it. To make an open white heart in a red square, you cut away the heart inside the outlines and leave the square area of the eraser standing around it. For the sake of example, let's say you choose to make a solid red heart to print on white paper. The general method suggested for carving the straight lines of the practice stamps can also be used in carving curves: keep the knife to the left of the lines, hold the knife at a slight angle, and cut toward yourself.

When cutting curved lines, it is a good idea to put a small square of paper underneath the eraser before you start. The carving will be easier to do if you turn the eraser slowly as you cut; the paper helps the eraser to turn smoothly.

To start carving, turn the eraser so that the indentation at the top of the heart is nearest you. Hold the knife at a slant, as you did when cutting the practice stamps. Begin your first cut at the right side of the base of the indentation. Once you've begun cutting, keep the knife point steadily *in* the eraser. When the line begins to curve a little, start turning the eraser with your free hand and continue the cut, guiding it by the slow turning of the artgum, until you reach the tip of the heart. This system of turning the eraser will produce a smooth continuous curve, and will give you good control of the knife. When one side of the heart is outlined with a slanted cut, turn the heart upside down again, start at the tip, and cut around

*To make a solid red heart, cut away the unshaded areas.*

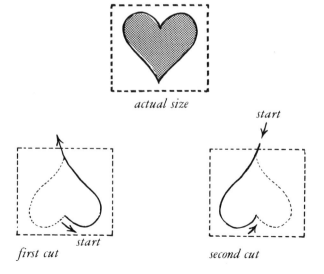

*actual size*

*first cut*

*second cut*

the other side of the design. Now form a groove all around the heart by making two slanting cuts to meet the outline cuts.

With a little practice you will find that cutting a curve is really quite easy. As you turn the eraser, carve slowly and continuously to the end of the line. If you lift the knife in the middle of a curved line, and stick it back into the rubber to continue the cut, the knife will often make a woggle at that point. So, as you work, even if the phone rings, don't stop to answer it—keep on cutting until you reach a point where you must stop anyway, or where the line of the design changes direction. Proceed with the valentine stamp as you did with the practice stamps: cut another groove around the first, clear away the background, make trial proofs, and keep on clearing away the background until you have a perfect print.

*Planning and Printing Your Valentine*

Once you have cut your valentine stamp, you need to decide on the approximate size and shape of your greeting card. If your design unit is small, as it is in this case, the area around it should not be too large. If your valentine is to be mailed, you must also select an envelope and plan your card to fit it. You can use a plain stiff card, or you can use paper and fold it in one of the ways shown in the drawings. Or you can

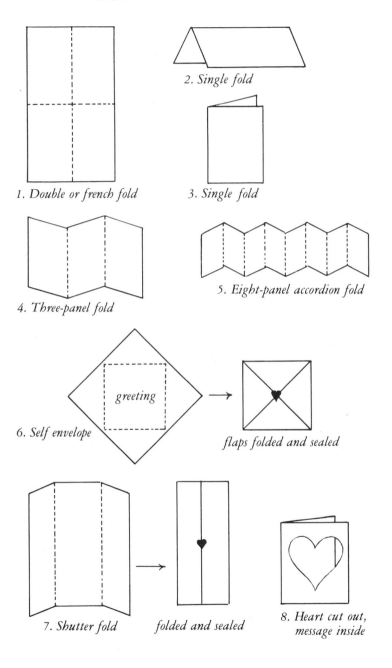

1. Double or french fold

2. Single fold

3. Single fold

4. Three-panel fold

5. Eight-panel accordion fold

6. Self envelope

greeting

flaps folded and sealed

7. Shutter fold

folded and sealed

8. Heart cut out, message inside

experiment with cutting and folding sheets of scratch paper to see if you can devise a way to seal the paper with a heart stamp so that no envelope is necessary. Or perhaps you will prefer to make your own envelope out of white, pink, or red paper. The drawing shows you how to put your valentine in the center of a sheet of paper and draw the lines for cutting out

## HOW TO MAKE AN ENVELOPE

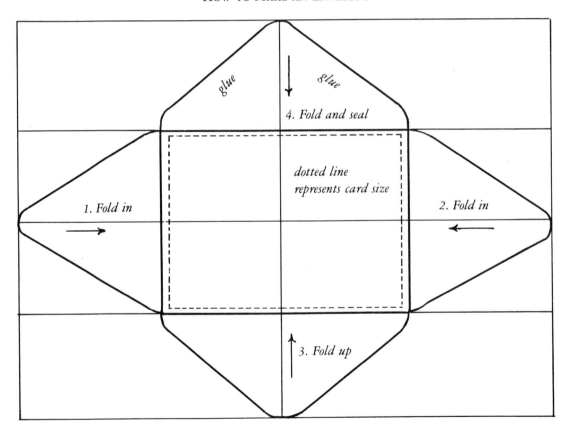

glue

glue

4. Fold and seal

dotted line represents card size

1. Fold in

2. Fold in

3. Fold up

an envelope for it. Paper for an envelope needs to be more than twice as wide and twice as long as the card.

On the folded and cut papers, try printing your stamp in different ways. After you have decided on an arrangement, or layout, as designers call it, think up what you want to say. Practice lettering or writing the message with the red felt pen so that you can allow the proper space for it in your layout. The possible combinations of hearts and lettering are almost endless.

Always make a preliminary trial impression of a stamp on scratch paper before you print it on good paper for the first time. The first inking of a clean dry stamp may not always print perfectly. The second inking, and those that follow, usually make better impressions.

When you have decided upon a layout you like, measure, mark off carefully, and cut your paper to the right size. If you are using pencil guidelines for your writing or stamping, rule and mark the lines lightly with a soft pencil. After printing, let the ink dry for five minutes or so; then you can erase the pencil lines without harming the impression. To print hearts in a circle, use a compass or, with a pencil, draw around a round cup or dish. Practice printing the hearts just inside the outer rim of the circle, with all the tips pointing toward the center. Ink the stamp well for each impression. The little stamp with the ¾-inch heart prints exactly twelve times, positioned like the numbers on the face of a clock, inside a circle that is 4 inches across.

A simple arrangement of hearts and written message placed so as to leave a comfortable margin around the page looks a little neater than a helter-skelter layout. But it also looks more formal. Feel free to express your own ideas and style. The fun in printing is in doing exactly what you want to.

February is not the only month of the year when your heart stamp will come in handy. You can use it to decorate stationery, for example. Or you can print some hearts and cut them

My heart beats only for you.
Please be my Valentine!

out, then use the cutouts as seals or stickers to put on the flaps of envelopes, to hold folded cards together, or to decorate gift packages. Chapter 10 in this book shows you several ways to print patterns for gift-wrapping papers and box covers, using the same little heart stamp and a couple of new versions of it.

# A Printing Trick

*After you have carved a stamp, and before you begin to print with it, use a ball-point pen to mark an arrow on the back of the eraser, showing which end of the stamp goes UP.*

# ☞ Another good trick

*A useful thing to have is a 6-inch, 45-degree, clear plastic triangle, obtainable at art stores. This will guide you in marking off lines for true square corners or right angles when you are cutting out sheets of paper or cards. You can make yourself a cardboard triangle (less durable, but cheaper) from a stiff card. Choose a card at least 6 inches square with a right-angle corner. Measure off 6 inches from the corner on two sides of the card and make a pencil dot at each spot. Draw a line between the dots and cut across that line. Discard the rest of the card.*

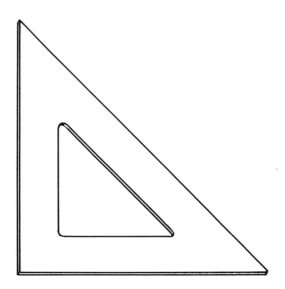

# 4. PRINTING WITH READY-MADE ALPHABET SETS

The neat, stamped letters printed from ready-made alphabet sets you can buy look more professional than handwriting, and printing with them is easy and quick. You can use any one of several kinds and sizes of rubber-stamp sets to print messages, greetings, poems, and stories. In addition to using commercially made sets, you can carve a few simple larger alphabet letters, traced from this book, in the same way you cut your first three designs. With these you can print monograms and initials. Or you can carve a whole alphabet of your own with which to print bookmarks, signs, posters, and labels. By combining professional-looking alphabet letters with your own handcut eraser-stamp designs, you will find there is almost no limit to the kinds of printed pieces you can turn out.

Of alphabet printing sets you can buy there are two distinctly different kinds: the small sets sold in toy stores and hobby shops, and the more complete and expensive office stamp-printing outfits. The two vary greatly in style, quality, and price.

*Printing Sets from Toy and Hobby Shops*

The alphabet printing sets that cost from ninety-eight cents to three or four dollars in toy departments are supposedly ready for use, but in most cases, such a proclamation on the box is misleading—to say the least. Anyone who tries to turn out good printing with such a set will surely run into trouble. The flat letters cast on rubber—sometimes plastic—squares are often less than ¼ inch thick and are therefore hard to handle. Even the more expensive of these sets, nicely boxed for hob-

byists, with miniature stamp pads and a bottle of ink, sometimes have rubber or composition letters that are so thin they
are very difficult to hold. And it is impossible to press them
on the stamp pad and print impressions from them without
leaving finger marks on the paper—to say nothing of the ink
left on your fingertips.

Another problem is that most of the inexpensive sets have
only capital, or upper-case, letters and numerals, with sometimes some punctuation marks and a few little decorations.
They have no small, or lower-case, letters. (The terms *upper
case* and *lower case,* by the way, are derived from the old
containers for metal type in printshops. In these, the letters
were distributed in small compartments with the capital letters
in the *upper* and the small letters in the *lower* part of the
wooden tray or case.)

Still, the unmounted letters in some of these cheaper toy
sets are quite sharp and well designed, and fortunately there
is a way to make them serviceable. Most of the greeting cards
in this book were printed with letters from toy sets. The
procedure for making the letters usable takes a little time and
care, but it is worth the trouble because it will save you quite
a bit of money; the prices for the more expensive office printing sets start at about fifteen dollars. Making the thin letters
useful is simple: paste the letters on a wooden stick, saw the

mounted letters apart, and presto! you have an alphabet printing set with each letter on its own square "handle" of wood. The mounted letters are easy to hold and will print very well. A little later in this chapter, you will learn exactly how to mount the letters.

Six examples of letters printed from toy sets, with the ornaments that sometimes come with them, are illustrated and described below. (All are shown actual size.)

# NEAT UPPER CASE 1 2 3 4

The letters in the first row above were cast on thin rubber squares that had to be taken apart and mounted on wood. They are from a set called Hong Kong Phooey, and the box advises you to "make your own comic strip." The small characters for the "strip," below the letters, are cast on thin plastic rectangles with small handles. The set costs about three dollars.

# ADMISSION 25¢

### SUCH TINY LETTERS!
### IN A HOLDER 1 2 3

The letters in the three rows above are from a rather elaborately boxed toy set called Sign and Ticket Shop. The large open letters and figures come individually mounted on small wooden handles, ready for use. The tiny letters (for printing tickets, we suppose) are cast on $\frac{1}{8}$-inch cubes of rubber to be set or squeezed into the channels of a wooden holder that can stamp up to four lines of printing at one time. A small pair of tweezers and a lot of patience are required to use them. The set is made by the Superior Marking Equipment Co. (see Sources of Supply), and the cost is about four dollars.

The two rows of letters and numbers below are printed from toy sets made in the Orient and distributed in the United States. The letters are not especially well designed, but are just goofy enough—particularly the numerals—to be rather amusing. Each set contains an assortment of ornaments, some of which are shown below and on page 45. A number of the little designs are already mounted on wooden handles, ready for use; those that are not will have to be glued to wood. The price of such an imported set runs from four to six dollars.

# CAPITALS 123

# UPPER and lower

The Happy Birthday letters and the numerals and symbols on page 46 came in cast-rubber strips, packaged on a small card, beneath a plastic bubble. All of them had to be mounted on wood, but they are a very useful size and quite well designed. You will note that this set has been used very often for the greeting cards shown in the illustrations. This set was

# HAPPY BIRTHDAY

# ★ 8 9 10 × + = ? % "

the biggest bargain anyone will probably ever find—ninety-eight cents. It was bought at a toy shop.

*A special note about numerals:* If you have bought one of the toy printing sets and the number *9* seems to be missing, it has not been included because the number *6* can be turned upside down and used to print a *9.* In the same way, if there is no zero, you can print *10* by using number *1* and the letter *0.*

*How to Mount Alphabet Letters on Wood*

When you buy one of the toy printing sets with very flat letters, you will probably find that the letters are loosely fastened together in strips. They are scored so that you can pull them apart. To mount the letters on wood, you will need the following simple materials:

Ruler and pencil

Stick of soft wood about 28 to 30 inches long by ½ inch wide by ½ inch thick. Shops that sell models and modelmaking supplies sell 24-inch-long basswood sticks in the right thickness, so you will need two lengths. Soft pine will also do.

Epoxy glue

Handsaw. Any one of these will do: a small cross-cut saw, a dovetail saw, or backsaw. The thinner the blade, the easier the saw will be to use; a dovetail or backsaw is therefore preferable.

Small wooden miter box *or* a 2-inch metal C-clamp (a miter box is easier to use).

Sandpaper. You will need a small piece of fine sandpaper.

From your household: a piece of scrap wood about 24 inches long; a felt pen; a small flat cardboard box with a lid, in which to store your printing set, and four or five ½-inch-wide strips of wood or corrugated cardboard to fit in the box as dividers for the rows of letters.

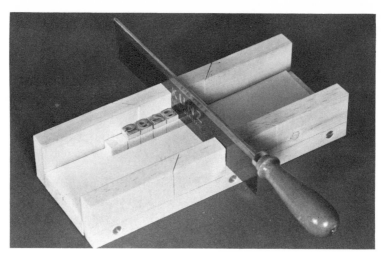

*Miter box with dovetail saw.*

The first step is to glue your letters and numbers to the wood stick with the epoxy glue. Once they are mounted, there are two methods you may use to cut the letters apart. If you are going to use a saw in a miter box (see photo), it is all right to glue them all on one long stick. If you have no miter box and therefore intend to use a C-clamp to hold the wood while sawing, it is better to glue your letters on about three shorter lengths of the ½-inch by ½-inch stick, being sure to leave about an inch at the left end of each stick (as you read the letters), in order to have a space on which to set the C-clamp.

Now you need to find out how much space to leave between the letters for the saw blade. To determine this, use your saw to make a shallow trial cut straight across the piece

*C-clamp*

of scrap. The width of the cut will be very small, but look at it closely because it roughly represents the amount of space you must leave between each of the letters as you glue them to the stick. Plan to leave a little *more* than this space—never less. Now pull your letters apart and spread them out on the table in alphabetical and numerical order.

*Gluing the Letters to the Stick*

Read the directions on the tubes of epoxy glue and use the tab on the tube to mix on a square of paper two small equal-size dabs of glue from each tube. Do not mix a lot of glue, or it will dry before you are ready to use it. With the tab on

*49*

the tube, spread the glue thinly on about 6 inches of the stick and put the first of the rubber letters in place. If you are using a C-clamp, don't forget to leave room for it at the left end of the stick. Line the squares up straight on the wood and press them down lightly. Leave a slot between the letters that is wide enough to accommodate your saw blade. Mix and spread a little more glue and stick on more letters, a few at a time. Check them to be sure each one is perfectly aligned with the edge of the wood. If the space between the letters is too small, the saw blade will flip the letters off if it touches them. If you get epoxy on your fingers, wash it off promptly with soap. Allow the glue to dry about *twice* as long as the directions on the tube specify. Test one of the last letters applied by wiggling it to see if it is really firm. Wait a little longer if it is not. Once the glue is completely dry, you are ready to saw the letters apart.

*Using the Miter Box*

This simple gadget is made in such a way that a slot has already been cut straight across the two sides of the open wooden box to guide your saw in making straight cuts. To use the box, place the stick with the mounted letters up and with the first gap between the letters aligned with the slot in the miter box.

Hold the wood tightly against the back wall of the box with your left hand. Set the saw carefully in the slot and saw the letters apart slowly. As, one by one, they are cut, lay them out on the table in alphabetical order again.

### Using the C-Clamp

If you are using this device, which is tightened with a screw winder, the first preliminary step is to draw straight lines down the sides of your sticks exactly in the center of the little gaps between the letters. You can then follow these marked vertical lines for making straight-down cuts. To protect your worktable while sawing, put the scrap wood under your marked stick and clamp both pieces of wood to the table. Set the clamp on the left end of the stick. Place the wood near the front edge of the table. The penciled vertical lines should face toward you, and the letters should be *up.* Steady the stick with your left hand, and start sawing the letters apart at the right end of the stick, away from the clamped end. Work toward the clamp. Set the saw blade carefully into each little slot, being careful not to touch the rubber letters with the saw-teeth. Saw straight down and once a cut is started, do not lift or wiggle the saw. Place the cut-apart letters on the table in alphabetical order.

After all the letters have been cut apart—by either method —hold each letter in your hand and use a small piece of fine sandpaper to smooth off the ragged edges of the wood. Each little cube should be sharp-edged and clean. Don't touch the letters or your fingernails with the sandpaper! Blow off the dust.

*Marking and Storing Your Alphabet Set*

Don't become discouraged at this point—you are about to complete a perfectly good printing set that started out in useless condition! Mark with a felt pen on the wood end of each little cube the alphabet letter to which it is glued. Be sure to draw the letter right side up, to correspond with the rubber letter. Ink the letter and make a trial print from it if you are not sure which way it goes. Mark a small arrow pointing upward alongside the drawn letters showing where the top of the letters *N, S, H,* and *Z* come. Often there is a difference between the top and the bottom of these letters.

Keep your marked stamps in a small box, arranged in alphabetical order, with the rubber printing surfaces down and the labeled wooden ends up. If you toss your letters into a box in a jumble, far too much time will be required to find each letter when you need it for printing. Find (or buy at a five-and-dime) a little box about the right size to hold the set. It is helpful to glue little ½-inch strips of wood or corrugated cardboard to the bottom of the box between the rows of letters. This ½-inch space makes it much easier to get your fingers around a letter when you want to use it.

A box of letters should always be covered when not in use, to keep the dust out. If you put a rubber band around the box and its top, you'll be less likely to spill and scramble the letters. When professional printers use metal type, they occasionally spill it, and they have a special word for scrambled type—*pi*—pronounced like apple *pie.* When a printer has to confess that he *pied* his type, he is greatly embarrassed!

After your alphabet letters are boxed and ready for use, print a proof of the whole set, lining up the letters neatly in rows across a piece of paper cut to fit the top of the box. This label will help you to identify the sizes and shapes of the letters, and can be referred to when measuring the spacing of words and messages whenever you are planning to use the set. After you have printed the letters, don't forget to stamp off every trace of ink.

*Printing Sets from Stationery and Office-Supply Stores*

The set shown in the photograph on page 55 consists of well-designed small letters neatly arranged in a box. The letters are about $\frac{1}{4}$ inch high and are cast on rubber cubes about $\frac{5}{16}$ inch deep. With this set comes a wooden holder with a single narrow metal channel on the face of the printing surface. Letters can be set into the channel to make a line about 4 inches long, and the line can be inked and printed in one stamping. There is also a wider holder with four metal channels into which rows of letters can be set to print a four-line message or label.

Besides the very neat upper- and lower-case letters, this set also has numerals and punctuation marks. It is called Atlas

Makurown office rubber-stamp printing outfit No. 4—size 5A, 6a font, 24-point. It is a useful set to have, especially if you plan to print a number of pieces that are all alike—such as mailing labels or Christmas cards. The set costs about fifteen dollars. Here is how the letters look:

# Letters in a holder

The office rubber-stamp printing outfit shown in the photograph below, which is very complete and easy to use, costs from ten to sixteen dollars, or even more, depending on the size of the letters. Each letter in this kind of set is carefully mounted on its own little piece of shaped and varnished wood, and each is also labeled. The set consists of upper- and lower-case letters; it has complete numerals and punctuation marks, and an assortment of such useful symbols as fractions, stars, and hands. The upper-case letters in such sets range from about ⅛ to ¾ of an inch in height. This kind of set is not often carried in stock by office-supply stores, and will probably have to be selected from a catalog and ordered for you by the store. One good brand is called Superior Sign-Marker Set, No. 916—made in the United States by S. M. E. Co. (Supe-

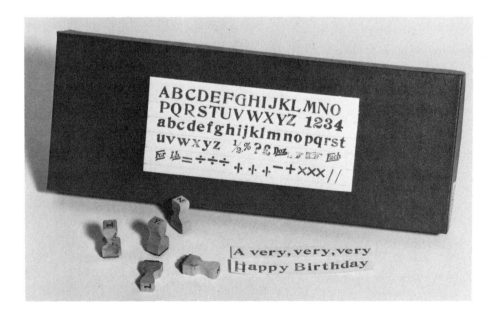

rior Marking Equipment Co., Chicago, Ill. 60613, who are also makers of toy printing sets). One catalog where these sets are listed is the *Crown Marking Products Catalog.* Here is an example of one style and the assortment of stamps:

# Very sharp letters

Sets like the office outfits just described are listed in manufacturers' or distributors' catalogs under Rubber Stamps as Sign-Marker Sets. (See the Sources of Supply section at the back of this book.)

We might explain here that ready-made rubber letters are listed in the catalogs in terms of *point size,* which is printers' lingo. Here is what a few of those sizes mean in inches: 12-point letters (or size 12) are about $\frac{1}{8}$ inch high; 14-point letters are a little less than $\frac{3}{16}$ inch high; 18-point letters are $\frac{3}{16}$ inch high; and 24-point letters are $\frac{1}{4}$ inch high. Catalogs often picture examples of the styles of letters, to help you make a selection.

If you buy an office printing set with letters that are ready for use, it will come in a nice sturdy box, but you should make a proof-sheet label to fit on the box top, showing all the contents—as suggested for the toy sets mounted on wood.

Still another kind of ready-to-use stamps with wooden handles can be bought at office-supply stores. You may not have much use for them, but perhaps you will want to investigate them. They carry all kinds of phrases needed in business offices, such as "Confidential," "Please Expedite," "Overdue," "Paid," and similar warnings and labels. Also, if you want to make a black-and-white drawing of any insignia or phrase you plan to use often, you can have a rubber stamp made from it photographically. Custom-made stamps, including name and address stamps, are rather expensive but handy.

## Hand-Carved Alphabets Made of Erasers

If the letters of ready-made toy or office printing sets seem too small and delicate for some of the printing you want to do, you can carve your own alphabet set. It will be useful for projects like signs and posters that require large bold letters that are intended to be seen at a distance.

The alphabet shown opposite is composed of simply designed letters about $1\frac{1}{16}$ of an inch in height. They are easy

ABCDEFGHIJ

KLMNOPQRS

TUVWXYZ-&

abcdefghijklm

nopqrstuvw

xyz !?.,;:

1234567890

to carve. In Chapter 6 there is another alphabet that has even bolder and slightly larger letters. The letters in both alphabets require only straight cuts, and you can trace them directly from this book. The letters in the first alphabet were planned to fit very economically onto the large 1½- by 3-inch Mars white erasers. To make the whole alphabet requires about six large Mars erasers, but if you plan to print only a monogram or a set of initials, carve only enough erasers for the number of letters you need.

Most of the procedure will be familiar to you. Trace the letters from the book very carefully, protecting the page with your acetate plastic sheet, and using a ruler to mark off guidelines for each line of letters. Prepare whatever number of erasers you need by ruling and cutting off the ¹⁄₁₆-inch edge on both sides of their length. Then measure carefully and draw a pencil line down the exact center of the length.

Transfer the traced letters—in reverse!—to the eraser in two rows, fitting them against the edges and placing them very close together as shown in the drawing. Move and place your tracing for each letter so that no waste space is left between the letters.

After transferring the letters, cut the eraser in two lengthwise with one steady slice of the butcher knife against a wooden board. Then carefully cut all the letters apart, making

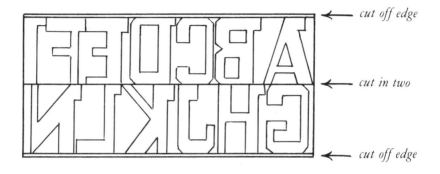

a single straight-down cut *exactly* on the dividing line each time. If you don't cut accurately on the lines, you will find yourself ending up with some fat and some thin letters.

Now carve out each letter in turn with the X-Acto knife, making continuous, straight cuts as much as possible. You will be surprised at how little work there is to do when both sides and the top and bottom of the letter have already been cut. Make a trial proof of each letter as you go along, correcting the cutting until you have a perfect print. If you spoil a letter, do it over again on a fresh eraser.

Mark the back of each finished letter with a ball-point pen —it works better on rubber than a felt pen. Store your hand-carved letters in a covered box, with ½-inch dividers between the rows. Stamp a neat box-top label showing all the letters, punctuation marks, and numerals in the set. You will need the proof for future reference.

Now that you know nearly everything about alphabet sets, you can try printing something with your letters.

# ★A PRINTING TRICK★

*After you have printed with ready-made alphabet letters several times, you may find that the edges and some of the open corners of certain letters have gradually picked up a coating of ink from the stamp pad. This accumulation of ink cannot be "stamped off." It should be wiped off gently with a soft, dry cloth. Sometimes you can eliminate these troublesome little areas by carefully carving them off. Letters with such open corners are capital I, L, T, V, W, and Y.*

# 5. BOOKMARKS AND BOOKPLATES

A neat little strip of card printed with a name or initials, or perhaps with initials and a design, makes a fine bookmark. You will need the same basic tools and materials listed in Chapter 1, plus an alphabet set. Any good-quality, rather stiff paper or card in white or a pale color will do. One particularly good brand of paper, which can be found in art stores, is called Strathmore Art Papers, 300 Series. The paper comes in assorted colors in packages of forty 9- by 12-inch sheets. Some of the sheets in the package are too textured to use, but others are smooth. The 45-degree plastic triangle or card described at the end of Chapter 3 will be useful for marking off cards and lining up lettering.

The bookmarks shown in the illustrations will give you

# MY OWN BOOKMARK

some ideas for using your alphabet set. They are printed with an assortment of sizes of letters you may not have, but any printing set with letters from ¼ inch to ⅜ inch in height can be used. Should you decide to carve a decorative design or initials, its width will determine the width of your bookmark. The length of your line of letters will determine its length. Drawings for the symbols shown may be traced and trans-

*actual size*

ferred to an eraser to be carved, or you can devise your own original designs. The bookmarks can be printed in whatever colors of ink you want, and on plain or colored paper as you choose. A simple decoration originally cut for a bookmark can be used over and over again and printed in several colors for all kinds of different projects. In designing your bookmark, stamp trial proofs on scratch paper to help you space and line

*actual size*

This page is where
Richard is reading

 HAS GONE THIS FAR

up your lettering. It is best to print your bookmark on a larger card and to cut it out after printing.

*Printing a Bookplate*

To make a bookplate, you need first a good idea, then all the basic materials mentioned before, and any good lightweight paper.

A bookplate is simply a small, neatly printed label that is pasted inside the front of a book to show the name of the owner. Designers of these little markers use handsome initials and symbols to identify a book in a distinctive way, sometimes illustrating a person's profession or hobby, and sometimes making a play on words of a person's name. Only a few years after Gutenberg's invention of movable type in Germany, the famous fifteenth-century English printer named William Caxton designed and made his own set of metal type. He also designed delicate ornaments and borders to accompany his elegant lettering. His type and designs were used in 1474 for one of the first books ever printed in England; they were also used to print bookplates for British collectors up to the eighteenth century.

Shown below is William Caxton's own bookplate with his initials on either side of an insignia that has never been deciphered. On the right are six lines which were printed using Caxton's Type 5. The lines first appeared in a book, *Doctrine of Sapience,* published in 1489.

Now late vs beþl
œ by pitie. ho w the
fone of god wold fuffre
for vs. how wel that we
may not wryte all. Ne
uertheles fome thyng we

You can print modern bookplates for yourself or for someone else by combining initials or a name with a carved rubber-stamp design. It will not have the fine details that Caxton could make by printing from metal, but it can have a distinctive twentieth-century look about it, and it will serve its purpose equally well.

Most books nowadays come wrapped in paper book jackets —these were unknown when books were bound in fine leather—so your bookplate will have to be pasted on the book's flyleaf, where it can be seen. The bookplate itself should not be too large; the size of your letters and ornaments will determine its dimensions. Here, again, you can use more than one color of ink, if you wish.

*actual size*

# A PRINTING TRICK

*If you want to print letters in a straight line, you will find a guide stick useful. To make the stick, cut a piece of wood about ½ by ½ by 6 inches. To find out exactly where to draw the guideline on which to set the stick, ink the capital letter E from your alphabet. Make an impression on paper, but do not pick up the stamp. Hold it in place and mark a pencil line on the paper along the lower edge of the mounting of the stamp. Lift the stamp, and extend the line the length of your line of lettering. Hold the guide stick on the line and set all the rest of the stamps against it. If this seems complicated, try printing a short word using only a drawn guideline.*

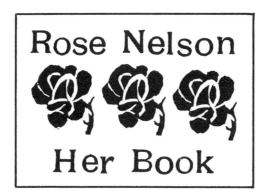

# ☞ Another good trick

*When printing with an alphabet, whether you are using all upper-case letters or both upper- and lower-case letters together, the spaces left between words should be about the same as the width of the capital letter E. When you need to estimate the space required to print a few words, use the printed alphabet pasted on the box lid of your printing set as a guide. Count each letter in the line you are planning to print as one character, and also count the spaces between the words as one character. Now count off the same number of characters in your alphabet proof, measure the length of that number of characters, and this will tell you how many inches of space are needed to print the line.*

This book
belongs to
THE ADAMS
Ann & Robin

# 6. POSTCARDS, NOTEPAPER, SIGNS, POSTERS, AND LABELS

Here are five more kinds of things you can print with an alphabet lettering set and carved eraser decorations. One or more of them may hit your needs right on target. Do you want some distinctive postcards? Would you like to have some personalized stationery? Could your church group or club use a poster? Each of these projects can turn out to be really interesting to do, and very useful, too.

Any poster or sign will probably be larger in size than the pieces you have been printing up to now. But in some ways, the more space you have to work in, the more freedom you have in planning your lettering and design. Here is a chance to use some offbeat arrangements. Keep in mind, though, that every design needs careful planning, even one with funny illustrations or lines of tipsy lettering.

The tools and materials for these projects are the same as usual—see Chapter 1.

*Postcards*

You can make your own postcards from the many kinds and colors of stiff paper available at art stores. Government postcards measure 3½ by 5½ inches. You can cut your cards to that size, or you can vary those dimensions a little and still mail cards at the regular postcard rate. If cards are as much as an inch larger each way, however, they will usually require letter postage. Postcards can be printed on either the message or the address side, but be sure to leave enough open space for the handwriting. Most of the examples shown in this book are printed

*actual size*　　　　　*A flower made up of stems and leaves and a design from Chapter 5.*

in two colors, and they will start you thinking of designs of your own—so that when anyone sees your postcard, he or she will know it is from *you.*

*Notepaper*

Your own stationery or notepaper can be marked with initials or with ornaments of various kinds. The illustrations show a few of the ways initial letters can be used, and especially how

good morning

*actual size*

good morning

*actual size*

stamped designs can transform a box of plain, inexpensive stationery into very handsome-looking writing paper. A bird, a heart, a rooster, a cat, or a flower will give your paper identity. You can also print notepaper to give to a friend. It makes a very unusual and welcome present.

Some alphabet-set letters are too large and too bold for printing a whole name and address on stationery, but you will probably want to avoid using the conventional kind of commercial printing that can be ordered from your neighborhood stationery store.

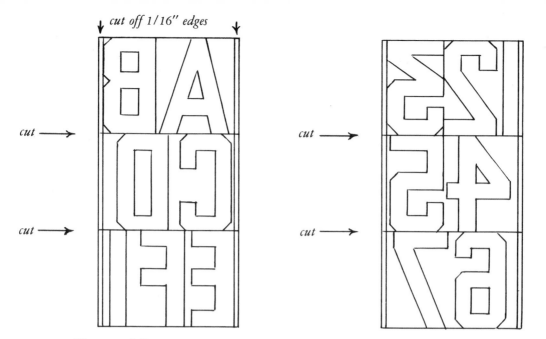

*Signs and Posters*

Everyone needs signs—from the snappy "Out to Lunch" to the personal "This Is Eddie's Room—Keep Out." The larger-size letters shown on page 76 and the slightly smaller-size letters in Chapter 4 are suitable for posters and signs. Your alphabet-set letters may be too small.

To make the large alphabet set, first cut off the edges of the long sides of your erasers. Draw lines across each eraser as shown, 1 inch apart, and transfer the letters to the erasers—in reverse. Use a butcher knife to cut each eraser into three pieces. Then cut the letters apart and use the X-Acto knife to carve each letter.

ABCDEFG

HIJKLMN

OPQRSTU

VWXYZ&

1234567

890?!|.',

When you are ready to make a poster or large sign, you can print on the white cardboard that comes back from the laundry inside clean shirts. Or you can buy bristol board or poster board in stationery, variety, school-supply, and art stores. These boards come in 22- by 28-inch sheets in white and various colors and usually cost less than fifty cents a sheet.

It's a good idea to make a rough preliminary print of your design on scratch paper. If you find you have a great deal of information to put on a sign, use carved stamps and rubber alphabets to print the decorations and the most important lines of the text. Then add the rest of the information in a block, lettering it by hand with a colored felt pen.

You have one big advantage over a commercial printer, who charges for each printed color—you can use as many as five colors of ink on a single poster, if you wish, at almost no extra cost!

When making a poster, it's a good idea to print the whole design on scratch paper. This will help you plan the amount of cardboard you will need. On this test print you don't have to be careful to measure off and place everything exactly where it will finally go. When you are ready to print the final poster, you can use each line of the trial proof to space the final print accurately. The method is this: mark off light horizontal guidelines for each word on the final poster. Now cut

# NOTICE!
# Big Circus Sat.
# 10 A.M.
### Caldwell's back yard

# Tickets 10$^C$

*actual size*

out each separate word of the test printing. Lay the cutouts, each in turn, just above the area where the word is to be printed. The cutout strips of lettering will serve as your guides for spacing and placing the lettering on the poster.

## Labels

Hand-printed labels will keep things looking very neat all around the house. Labels are needed for storage boxes and containers in a workshop (10-penny Nails), in the basement (Christmas Tree Lights), in the attic (Father's Books), in a closet (Robert's Panama Hat), in drawers (Miscellaneous

Jewelry), in bedrooms (Sally's Junk), in a sewing room (Pinking Shears), on the kitchen shelf (Raisins), and in the garage (Salt for the Driveway).

If you look for places where labels are needed, you will find enough work to do to keep you busy printing quite a while!

*An Idea File*

Now that you have had some printing experience, you might like to start your own idea file. A good way to begin is to collect clippings from newspapers and magazines that will give you ideas for designs and decorations to carve for stamps.

Keep the clippings in a small folder. All professional artists and designers know the value of such a reference file. When you are reading a newspaper or magazine, look for simplified designs like hands, animals, birds, trees, butterflies, flowers, monograms, and so on. Good, distinctive trademarks made from letters or symbols are useful to have, too.

## A PRINTING TRICK!

*If silly or expressive words are printed in a wavy or jagged line, they may make the words of a riddle or joke even funnier, and they will attract attention to a poster or sign. Try printing the phrase "I truly love you" in a bumpy line.*

PETER'S ROOM

KEEP OUT

# 7. GREETING CARDS FOR ALL OCCASIONS

How many greeting cards do you suppose you receive in a year? And how many do you send? The occasions for sending cards come around often on the calendar:

> *New Year's Day*
> *Valentine's Day*
> *Easter*
> *Mother's Day*
> *Father's Day*
> *Hanukkah*
> *Christmas*

There are other special happenings during the year, and it is nice to send cards on these occasions, too:

*Birthday*
*Bon Voyage*
*Congratulations*
*Get Well*
*Party Invitations*
*Thank You*
*Wedding Anniversary*

A hand printer who designs his or her own cards, each one created for a particular occasion or person, can make the sending of greetings what it really should be—a unique gesture that is gracious and meaningful. You can also be sure nobody on your list will *ever* receive a card like the original ones you yourself design and print. And because greeting cards are so expensive these days, by printing your own, you will save more than a few pennies.

The materials you need to print greeting cards are about

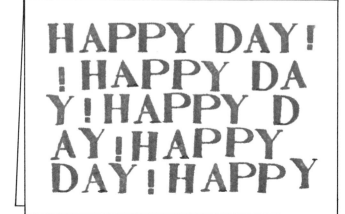

the same as those required for earlier projects. In making cards, you should give special attention to your choice of paper. With colored papers, for example, you can produce especially gay and attractive greetings. The paper need not be expensive. You can print on brown wrapping paper, for example, if you think it suits your design and the occasion. Some art stores carry Kraft (wrapping) paper, which comes in six or eight colors and costs only about twenty-five cents a square yard. It is not very heavy, but it can be used as a double or

*actual size*

*actual size*

French-fold card; and it is inexpensive enough to be made into envelopes in mix-or-match colors to accompany your cards. If you have stamp pads in four colors of ink—red, blue, green, and purple, as well as black—you will find lots of opportunities for colorful printing.

You will get ideas from the cards shown in the illustrations. Even if you have only one alphabet set, you can make a variety of greetings. Drawings for the decorative designs are given so that you can trace and carve them if you wish. To make the New Year's card, first trace the numerals in the drawing, transfer these to your card, and use the outlines as a guide for stamping the greeting, in whatever words you choose. The numerals can of course also be used for birthday cards. (Turn the 6 upside down to make a 9.) The drawings of the Easter egg and punctuation marks on page 89 may be traced and used in the same way.

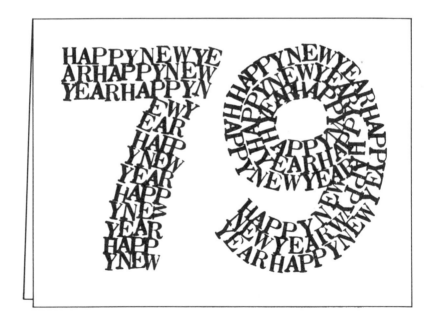

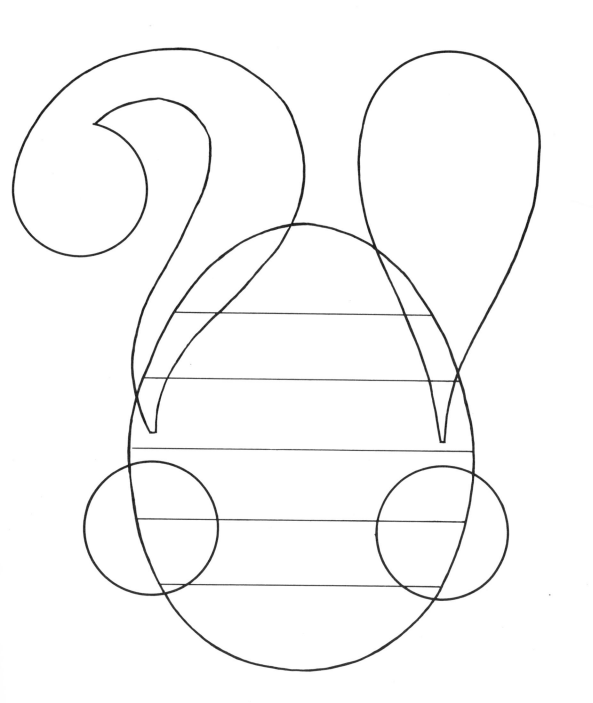

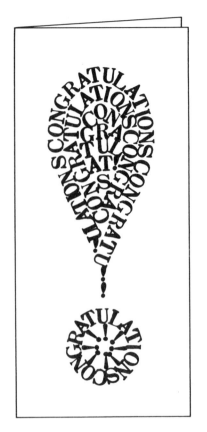

*Some Other Things to Know About Paper*

In stationery stores you can buy plain notepaper in many colors and sizes. Boxes of twenty or twenty-five folded sheets and envelopes sell for two to three dollars. These are a good choice if you are planning to print smaller greeting cards, and a whole box of them printed makes a fine gift.

Joyeux
Noël
*Michelle*

GREETINGS

Many art stores sell very elegant, rather large stiff cards, measuring about 4½ by 6 inches, with envelopes. These, though more expensive, are beautiful to send on very special occasions. One good kind is made by Strathmore. A packet usually contains ten or twelve cards and envelopes.

*actual size*

# HANUKKAH
# GREETINGS

Many of the printed greetings shown in the illustrations were printed on a small standard-size "announcement" card or folded sheet 3¾ by 4¾ inches. This sort of card is usually made of a good-quality white-vellum paper with an accompanying envelope, and most commercial printers can supply you with similar sets. You might have to buy a box of 250 or 500

*actual size*

sets, but this is an inexpensive way to buy paper, and it is always useful for your own letters and notes, whether printed or not. Don't forget to liven up your printing with different colored inks.

The drawings in Chapter 3 that show various ways of folding sheets to make a valentine will be a handy reference for you when you are planning to make greeting cards for other occasions.

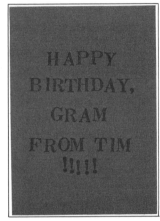

*actual size*

# 8. PRINTING
# TWO COLORS
# IN REGISTER

By using two or more colors of ink, you can often make your work more attractive than if you limit your printing to black or a single color. On each of the bookmarks shown in Chapter 5, for example, the name or design at the end was printed in one color and the long line of lettering in ink of a different color. The initials or decorations on the bookplates were also done in one color and the lettering in another. Some of the stationery in Chapter 6 was printed in the same way; the circus poster was stamped in four colors of ink.

If you will look carefully at the illustrations of each of these, you will see that the second or additional colors are not very close to, and not actually an integral part of the same design unit as the first or other colors. So, printing these pieces is simply a matter of stamping one color first, then adding the second by eye, or by marking the spot where the second unit belongs, and stamping it more or less where it should go. This is a very simple way of making a multicolor print.

But you can also print a two-color design in which the colors are interdependent—they form a complete unit. Colors that are related to each other in this way in the *same* design unit must print in exactly the same position; or must be "in register," as printers say. Each color is an indispensable part of the design. If one color were printed out of position—even if only very slightly—the design would be deformed. And if one of the colors were taken away, the design would be incomplete and obviously missing something.

The specific example that follows will show you how two-color register works. Since the design has some rather small delicate details, you should use two large white Mars erasers, one for each color. Artgum would be too crumbly for this fine a carving. Besides the two erasers, the only thing required in addition to the basic items in Chapter 1 is a small gadget that will act as a right-angle guide for registering the colors. This L-shaped or right-angle guide can be cut from a piece of pine or basswood ½ by 1½ by 2 inches. You will need a saw and either a miter box or a bench vise to hold the wood while you cut it. If you have no way to saw out the small piece of wood, you can substitute for it an inexpensive 1½-inch metal corner brace, available at most hardware stores.

*Making the Owl Valentine*

The valentine in the photograph shows a little owl printed in two colors from two matching stamps.

The owl has a red body and black eyes, beak, and feet. You can see that if one of the colors were printed out of position, the design would look cockeyed, and if one of the colors were taken away, the design would not be complete. The question is, how do you manage to print the red body from one stamp, then print the black parts from another stamp in exactly the right places to put the whole owl together? To print the two in perfect register, you need a foolproof way of controlling the placement of the two inked stamps.

*actual size*

Here is the procedure. First, trace the complete design on tracing paper—the body of the owl, the outlines of the eyes, beak, and legs—and trace the dotted line around the owl. You don't need to trace the heart or the square that represents the card.

Trim off the $\frac{1}{16}$-inch rounded edges of the long sides of the two erasers; then measure and mark a line across each of them to give you two stamps with a printing surface $1\frac{3}{8}$ by $2\frac{1}{4}$ inches.

Put the erasers on a cutting board and use a butcher knife to cut them crosswise on the guidelines. Discard the two ¾-inch pieces.

The design for each of the two colors—red and black—is to be transferred to, and then carved on, a separate eraser. Place your tracing of the owl facedown on one of the erasers and transfer by rubbing over *only* the lines of the *red* for the owl's body and around the eyes. Those are the only lines you need on this stamp. Now put the same tracing facedown on the second eraser and rub over *only* the circular lines for the black eyes and the lines for the beak and the legs. Now you have two erasers that are ready for carving.

Carve the designs on the stamps as accurately as possible, holding the erasers by their sides in order not to smudge the pencil transfers. Make separate trial proofs of each stamp, and do any necessary cleanup of the carving until both stamps print clean impressions. The large open area on the black stamp will have to be cut quite deeply in order not to pick up ink from the pad. In printing with it, you may find that after each use you have to wipe the stamp with a soft cloth to remove smudges of ink. Wide open areas of a carved eraser sometimes cannot be cut deeply enough not to pick up some ink.

Now comes the trick that makes it possible to print the two

colors in exact register with each other. Both stamps were drawn from the same tracing, so that if they have been accurately cut, the two prints must fit together correctly—if the stamps are put down in turn in exactly the right spot on the paper. How can you be sure of doing that? By using your right-angle printing guide.

If you have a miter box or a carpenter's bench vise and a handsaw, make your guide out of wood. Measure, mark, and cut off a rectangular piece of pine or basswood $\frac{1}{2}$ by $1\frac{1}{2}$ by

*The two stamps and the right-angle printing guide.*

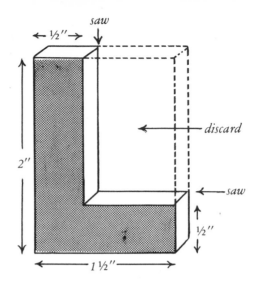

2 inches. Measure off and draw pencil lines on the cut rectangle as shown in the drawing to mark off an L-shaped right angle. Using the miter box or vise to hold the wood, make two saw cuts—one against the grain and one with the grain. Stop sawing where the two cuts meet. Discard the 1- by 1½-inch rectangle. Smooth all the cut surfaces of the L with a piece of sandpaper.

An alternative to a wood right angle is to buy a 1½-inch metal corner brace at a hardware store. This will also serve as a printing guide, but it is not quite as easy to use as the wooden guide. The inside corner of the metal brace is slightly rounded, and thus is not as sharp as the angle cut with a saw from wood. So, if you are going to use the metal angle, you will have to shave off the corners of your eraser stamps to

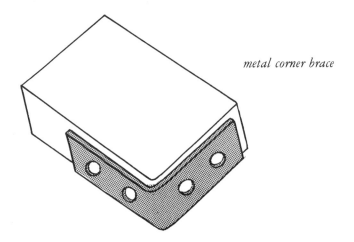

*metal corner brace*

make them fit snugly in the angle. On each stamp, the corner to cut is the one that will come at the *lower left* of the print when the stamp is facedown on the paper. Use the pocket-knife to round off that corner, working slowly and trying the stamp in the angle until it fits very snugly against the two inner sides of the metal and tightly in the corner, as shown in the drawing.

Both kinds of right-angle guides are used in the same way. With your two carved stamps at hand, and two stamp pads— red and black—you are ready to make a two-color trial proof. On a piece of scratch paper, draw two pencil lines at right angles to each other, where you want the bottom and the left-hand side of the stamps to print. This is what you would do if you were preparing to print the greeting card.

## Printing the Two-Color Owl

In color printing, it is a good idea to print the lightest color first and the darkest color last, particularly when, as in this case, one color must be printed over another. So start with red. Ink the owl stamp. Place the L-shaped guide on the pencil lines on the paper and hold it in place with one hand as you ease the inked stamp down firmly into the corner of the angle and onto the paper. Don't move the guide. Press down on the stamp to make the impression, then lay it aside but leave the guide in place. Ink the second stamp with black ink and press it into the angle guide and down onto the paper as you did the first stamp.

If all goes well and nothing has slipped, you will have a two-color design of a red owl with big black eyes, a beak, and feet exactly as they were drawn originally. Small variations in cutting will make minor differences, but since this is a hand operation, these small variations are quite natural and are to be expected.

After you have made two or three practice impressions, you will be able to handle the guide and the stamps quite easily. If you wish, you can experiment by printing with only pencil guidelines to see if you can register the two colors accurately. You may succeed in making an OK print, but you are likely

to have an owl casting its eyes to one side with its beak off-center! The advantage of the guide is that it ensures perfect register every time you print.

If you want to make the complete owl valentine shown in the photographs, first print the two-color owl and the message in the center of a small sheet of white paper. On another sheet of white paper, print the message for the inside of the card. Trace the outline of the heart from the diagram of the owl. Place the tracing facedown in the correct position on the first and then on the second of the already-printed sheets. Transfer the lines with a hard pencil. Cut out the two hearts. Measure, mark off, and cut out a sheet of red paper 4½ by 9 inches and fold it in half crosswise. Use any kind of white glue (Elmer's or Sobo, for example) to paste the hearts in the center of the front and the inside of the valentine. Press the valentine under some heavy books until the glue has dried.

*Printing the Two-Color Mother's Day Card*

You can use the same method to print the Mother's Day card shown in the photograph. This particular card has purple flowers and green stems and leaves. In this case, although the two colors must be registered carefully, one color does not print over the other.

Use two large white erasers, and to prepare them, cut away the rounded edges of the long dimension. Trace the entire design shown in the drawing. Transfer to one eraser *only* the flowers, and to the other *only* the stems and leaves.

The flowers will require the whole length of one eraser, but the stems and leaves will use only about 2¼ inches of length. After both parts of the design have been transferred to the erasers, and before you do any carving, draw a straight line across the "stems" eraser, just above the top of the design. With a sharp butcher knife cut off the unneeded ¾-inch portion. This is done so that the design more nearly fills the stamp, and thus will print better because there will be no large nonprinting area that might pick up ink from the ink pad. In

*Transfer only the
flowers to this stamp.*

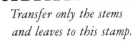

*Transfer only the stems
and leaves to this stamp.*

general, all stamps print better if the design fills as much of the four sides of the eraser as possible. A stamp with a very large open space at one end or on one side is a "rocker" and is hard to print. Of course, that circumstance cannot always be avoided—as with the black stamp for the owl, for example.

Now carve the two stamps, make trial proofs of them both separately, and clear the background as needed. Then use your L-shaped guide to print the purple (or some other color) blossoms and the green stems and leaves.

As you can see in the photograph, the two-color flower design was repeated three times in a straight row across the sheet of paper. The printed paper was then cut out to measure 4½ by 5⅛ inches. This was pasted on the front of a folded card made of a sheet of heavy green paper 5⅞ by 10¼ inches. With only two small stamps you can plant a whole garden of flowers across the card.

In making an interlocking-color design unit like the owl and the flowers, you also will have learned how to make a design with *three* colors and how to register them with an angle guide. But in designs that are only as large as our erasers, a third color does not add much to the final effect. Two colors printed on a third color of paper, or on white paper mounted on a colored card, will give you a bright and gay greeting.

# 9. SEWING TOGETHER A FOLDER OR BOOKLET

Here is another valentine you can make, and it is distinctive because of the way the pages are sewn together to make a folder or small booklet. The procedure, known as binding in professional terms, is nothing more than the process of attaching the pages to the cover. In this case, binding consists simply of taking two big stitches with a darning needle and a piece of heavy thread.

The photographs on the next page show the front cover and the inside pages of the sewn-together valentine. A heart-shaped opening has been cut in the front cover, through which the words on the first inside page can be seen, printed on white paper amid scattered flowers. A nineteenth-century version of a traditional verse has been printed on the third inside page.

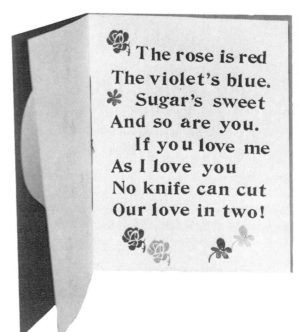

The rose is red
The violet's blue.
Sugar's sweet
And so are you.
If you love me
As I love you
No knife can cut
Our love in two!

To make the valentine, cut out two pieces of paper, 7 by 11 inches, and fold them together crosswise. Use a slightly heavier paper for the cover and any good-quality white paper for the inside pages. If the edges of the white paper show, trim them. Trace the drawing of the large heart, turn the tracing over, and transfer the outline to the center of the front cover. Cut out the heart. Fold the sheets together again and draw a light pencil line

*actual size*

on the first inside page, using the edge of the cutout as a guide. This line will help you in printing the page. Follow the photograph in printing the third inside page. When the ink has dried, fold the sheets together again, and you are ready to sew the valentine.

Fasten the cover and pages together with six paper clips. Open the folder and measure in 3½ inches from the edges

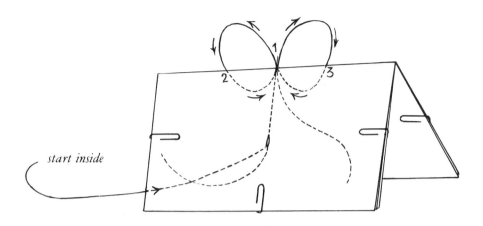

*start inside*

of the 7-inch dimension and make a pencil dot in the center
of the fold—shown as 1 on the drawing. Use the darning
needle to poke a hole through both sheets at that point. Close
the folder, and on the outside of the fold measure 1½ inches
in each direction from the center hole and make dots 2 and
3. With the needle, make a hole straight through the fold of
both sheets at these two places.

Thread the needle with a long piece of button or carpet
thread in a neutral gray or tan color. Start sewing from inside
the folder; push the needle through the center hole, pull up
the thread, but leave a 12-inch end inside the folder. Now sew
from the outside through hole 2 and pull up the stitch, but
keep hold of the 12-inch end inside. Sew out through the
center hole again, pull up the thread, sew into hole 3, and
remove the needle. Tie the two ends of the thread together

in a square knot at the center of the inside of the folder and cut off the ends of the thread. Remove the paper clips, and your valentine is bound together and finished.

You can print a small book and sew as many as five or six sheets of folded paper together in this same way. Be sure to make a rough sketch, or dummy, of the book first, and number the pages, so as to keep your text in order.

# A PRINTING TRICK

*Sometimes the upper-case letter I is set in the center of a square of rubber the same size as the other wider letters of the alphabet. This means that there is extra space on each side of the letter. In order to print the capital letter I in a word, you must always be careful to stamp it with the square quite close to the letter printed just before it. (Otherwise, there would be too much space on the left side of the I.) Then, the following letter can be placed the proper distance from the I; this will give even spacing and the line will read smoothly. Practice printing the phrase A PRINTING TRICK until you become familiar with how to handle that skinny letter I.*

# 10. PRINTING
# REPEAT PATTERNS

*Decorative Papers*
*for Gifts and Boxes*

By this time you probably have in your printshop quite a number of carved stamps. You may have ten or fifteen—or even as many as thirty. You can now use some of your stamps, or you can cut new ones, to print in yet another way. That is, you can make a *repeat* pattern by stamping one small design over and over again in different ways across a large area. These all-over designs can be used to make colorful gift wrappings for many occasions, as well as papers to cover boxes of all sizes. If you printed the Mother's Day card in Chapter 8, with its row of garden flowers, you already have made one small repeat pattern.

All of us are used to seeing such patterns in our everyday lives on things like wallpaper, dress and shirt materials, bed-

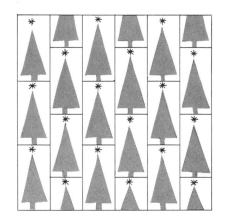

spreads and curtains. There are countless ways of repeating a design unit to make a pattern, and even if you limit yourself to the simplest of them, you can print some very attractive surface designs on paper.

The Christmas gift in the photograph is wrapped in paper printed with the small Christmas-tree stamp shown in Chapter 7. The design unit—the tree with its decorations—is printed in a common pattern called a *half-drop* repeat. The drawing shows how this kind of pattern is planned and why it has the name it does. The unit is repeated down the paper in a vertical row, but in the next row, instead of being printed exactly in line, the unit is moved down—or dropped—half of its vertical dimension below the unit in the first row. The background spaces between the printed units thus form a sort of second pattern that enhances the whole design.

The small square box in the next photograph is covered with yellow Kraft paper that has been printed with alternating green and red stylized flowers. These designs from Chapter 5 may be in your collection of stamps, also. The two flowers are printed in a *straight-line* horizontal repeat. But the units are moved one unit to the right in the row below, just to add interest to the pattern. The system works well in this case, because the units are similar although not exactly alike. The two flower units have been printed in reverse color from each other—one with a light background and one with a dark background. When exactly the same unit is used in this way, the pattern is called *counterchange* or checkerboard.

The design of triangles on the gift package in the same photograph was printed in alternating rows of blue and purple. First, one straight row of the unit of two little triangles was stamped across the paper. Then, directly under the first row, the stamp was turned upside down and printed straight across the paper in another horizontal row. You can see that the white stripe—which is nothing more than the space left between the two printed rows—becomes very important to the general effect of the pattern. This is also called a straight-

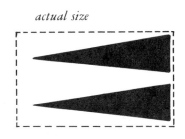

*actual size*

line repeat, although it is not necessarily true of all such repeats that the unit is flipped in this way. Sometimes the same unit is printed right side up, row after row. But however the unit is repeated, the spaces are always important. This is a good example of how one can create a handsome and sophisticated pattern by printing from a very small and simple geometric stamp.

The Christmas wrapping paper on page 116 was printed in green and blue; the more conventional green and red would, of course, be fine, too. This pattern is also a straight-line repeat, but because of the way it is designed, it gives the effect

*actual size*

of horizontal stripes. Although the last three patterns described are constructed on the same system, you can see that they do not look at all alike because of the differences in the design units.

The photograph on the next page shows a pattern printed on white paper with a red sun and a blue bird. The wrapped box is tied with royal-blue ribbon, and it bears a tag printed with the sun face. The sun stamp will be familiar to you from chapter 5. Although neither it nor the bird stamp was designed with a repeat in mind, they go well together because they are cheerfully related in style and subject matter. As shown in the drawing, they are printed horizontally in a straight-line repeat, but vertically, the birds have been moved to a position half to the right of the sun, making this a *brick repeat* pattern.

The smaller gift package in the same photograph is wrapped in a paper printed with a design taken from an abstract traditional motif. This is a true counterchange or

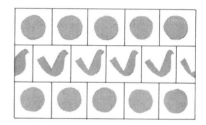

*actual size*

*actual size*

checkerboard pattern, with two identical units carved on one eraser, but one unit is white on a dark background, and the other is a dark unit on a white background. Printed in red and green, this is a Christmas paper, but printed in green and blue, green and purple, purple and blue, or black and one color, it can be used to wrap any gift.

Here are two ways to repeat two heart stamps to make quite different patterns. One is a counterchange pattern; the other, a straight-line repeat.

Or you can make heart stamps in a line design like the two shown on page 120, and use them alone or in combination with each other. Any of the patterns shown here could be used to make gift-wrapping papers or paper to cover a box for Valentine's Day. By adding a stem and printing the hearts in green, you can create a shamrock. Four hearts together make a flower; you may want to add a stem and a few leaves.

Experiment with the stamps you already have to create new patterns, or design some stamps of your own specifically for pattern printing. A repeat pattern should have some sort of order, and a consistent system of printing a unit or units. Of course there are also such things as *random* patterns; in making them, however, you should be careful that *random* does not turn out to be *confused!*

Don't overlook the possibilities of using your alphabet letters to print gift-wrapping paper, either with or without a carved stamp design. You can print a special greeting, a joke, a riddle, or simply a pattern made of appropriate words reading in all four directions. Stamp several trial proofs and see what you can come up with.

*Selecting and Printing Papers for Gift Wrapping*

A dull-surfaced paper is best for printing gift-wrapping papers. The paper should not be so heavy, however, that it will be difficult to fold around packages. Good-quality onionskin paper (if the sheet is large enough) is all right, but tissue paper is a little too thin and fragile.

Work on a large, open worktable where the sheets of paper can be spread out; have plenty of light. If you know that the sheet you plan to print is going to be used to wrap a small package, measure the box with a tape measure, and print a sheet that is only as large as you really need. Rule whatever guidelines are necessary to place your stamps, and to help you print the pattern straight with the edges of the paper. When you are stamping your pattern, do not attempt to leave straight plain margins on the sheets. Just continue to ink the stamp and print it (or part of it) right over the edge of the paper. Put a strip of brown paper underneath the edge to take the leftover part of the impression. This will save you any fussing about margins.

If you are going to use two colors, the methods are the same as for any printing: keep one stamp and its ink pad to the left of your sheet, and the pair for the other color to the right. And remember where they belong when you put a stamp down! The stamping of gift papers really goes quite fast. You can do a whole sheet in a surprisingly short time.

While you are printing the papers, print a gift tag to match. Use a small folded card cut so that the stamp fits neatly on it. Punch a hole in the upper left-hand corner of the tag for tying it to the package.


*Printing Paper to Cover Boxes*

Boxes covered with colorful papers can be used as containers for special gifts (and need no gift-wrap paper), or the boxes themselves make nice gifts to hold miscellaneous small treasures like jewelry, coins, and buttons. You can buy plain boxes in many sizes at Woolworth's and similar stores. Good-quality white or colored construction paper, Kraft paper, and many kinds of art papers are fine for covering boxes. The best kind of glue to use is any so-called white glue like Elmer's, Sobo, or Ad-A-Grip. It is not necessary to spread the glue over the entire surface of the box when applying the printed paper, but only along the inner edges of the box wherever the covering paper is turned in. A small, stiff glue brush is useful.

Papers to cover boxes are printed in the same way as gift-wrapping sheets. To find the size of the sheet of paper you need, use a tape measure, and follow this formula:

*The length of the box plus twice the depth plus 1 ½ inches equals the length of the sheet needed.*

*The width of the box plus twice the depth plus 1 ½ inches equals the width of the sheet needed.*

For example, a box 2 inches wide, 3 inches long, and 1 inch deep requires a sheet of paper 5 ½ by 6 ½ inches to cover it, leaving a little extra space all around. This will be enough paper to cover the bottom of the box, as well as the sides. Use the same formula to determine the size of the sheet you need to cover the lid. A lid is usually less deep than the box itself.

Now measure and cut your two sheets of paper. Measure, mark, and rule guidelines on both sheets. All boxes look better if the pattern is centered, so lay out your pattern starting in the exact center of the sheet, and rule off and mark with pencil all the guidelines you will need for printing. Print the two sheets and allow the ink to dry.

Once the stamped pattern has dried, you are ready to mark off and cut out the sheet so it will fit the box. The box and lid will be wrapped in the same way: you will cover the bottom as well as the sides of the box, and, of course, the top and sides of the lid.

Put the sheet to cover the box, printed side down, on the table and put the box, open side up, in the exact center of the sheet. Draw around the box. Put the box aside and use a ruler and pencil to extend the four lines in all directions out to the edges of the sheet. Next, measure the exact depth of the sides and mark and draw lines on all four sides for the depth of the box. On the diagram these are represented by the dotted lines that adjoin the central rectangle. Extend these lines out to the edges of the sheet. Measure, mark, and draw lines to add an edge $\frac{1}{2}$ inch wide on each of the sides. These edges will be folded in and pasted to the inside of the box.

Next, following the diagram, rule and draw the necessary slightly slanting lines for the cuts to be made on the flaps and fold-ins. It is these cuts that will allow you to place the paper neatly around the box. If you first use a sheet of scratch paper and follow the steps, folding that sheet around the box, then you can be sure that your sheet with the printed pattern will also fit well. When all the heavy cutting lines shown on the diagram have been drawn, cut out the sheet. (Ignore the dotted lines; they indicate only the folds.)

Now you are ready to paste the printed paper on the box. Set the box on the lines in the center of the sheet again. Have the glue handy in a small lid or dish, and follow the numbered steps on the diagram, 1 through 13, to fold and paste the cover sheet. Keep the paper pulled tightly around the box as you fold and paste, and always apply the glue only to the

# How to Cover a Box

11. *Fold in and glue*

4. *Fold around end of box; glue*

10. *Fold up end*

8. *Fold around end of box; glue*

3. *Fold in and glue*

2. *Fold up side*

1. *Set box in center*

6. *Fold up side*

7. *Fold in and glue*

5. *Fold around end of box; glue*

12. *Fold up end*

9. *Fold around end of box; glue*

13. *Fold in and glue*

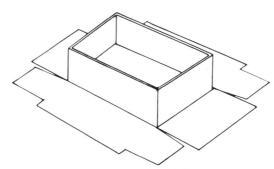

surface of the box, or to the already pasted-down flaps, not to the paper.

Cover the box lid in exactly the same way.

If you expect your box to be handled quite a lot, give both the lid and the box several coats of clear spray lacquer. Set the box and the lid separately on a square of cardboard. Work outdoors or in a well-ventilated room, and follow the directions on the spray can. Use the cardboard square to turn the pieces, and spray on several light coats of lacquer. The coating will be practically invisible, and it will help to protect the paper and keep it from becoming soiled.

One of the nicest parts of printing your own papers is that they will be unique. There is a kind of fascination, too, in seeing the pattern develop as you print. But there are other good points besides: your printed papers will cost about half as much as commercially printed gift wrappings, and at Christmastime this will be real money in your pocket. There is also every chance that your papers will be better looking than most of those you buy.

# 11. HOW TO COVER MEMO PADS, NOTEBOOKS, AND PORTFOLIOS

Inexpensive memo pads and notebooks of various kinds are, for some unknown reason, often quite dull and ordinary-looking. With very little effort you can transform these every-day, useful articles into attractive objects.

The portfolio in the photograph on the next page measures 8¼ by 10½ inches. It is covered with paper stamped in the flower design from Chapter 5 and the stem and leaves from Chapter 6, printed in a half-drop repeat pattern. The colors are red and blue on white paper; the cloth-tape hinge and lining are red. The stenographer's notebook on the right is covered in bright blue-green paper stamped in black; it is lined with black construction paper.

You can design and print similar papers to decorate date books, address books, albums, and portfolios of all sizes.

*actual size*

*Covers for Memo Books and Notebooks*

Many notebooks and memo pads are put together with a
metal wire binding at one side or end. Many have only the
manufacturer's name on the cover, and they look colorless
and utilitarian. These, as well as notebooks that are sewn
together and finished with a cloth or paper hinge, can be
covered with hand-printed papers for a whole new look.

If a notebook has rounded corners, which are hard to cover

neatly by folding paper around them, use the following simple method. Cut your decorative, hand-printed sheet so that it is about $\frac{1}{4}$ inch larger on all four sides than the notebook. Put some white glue (Elmer's or Sobo, for example) in a dish, and thin it with a few drops of water. Use a brush to mix it, and spread the glue evenly on the notebook cover. Put one edge of your printed sheet against the row of holes made for the wire binding, or against the tape binding. Let an extra $\frac{1}{4}$ inch of paper extend out over the other three sides of the notebook. Beginning at the binding, roll the sheet onto the glued surface, smoothing it hard with a soft cloth as you go to remove any air bubbles. Open the notebook out flat and apply the printed paper to the back cover in the same way. *Do not trim* the edges yet. Close the notebook and press it under heavy books overnight.

Once the glue is thoroughly dry, open the notebook and put the printed side of the front cover facedown on a piece of scrap cardboard. With one firm slow stroke of a single-edged razor blade, trim away the extra paper, using the edge of the cardboard notebook cover as your guide. Press down hard on the cover with your other hand as you cut. Of course you must be careful to keep your fingers out of the way of the blade! Cut straight past the rounded corner, then go back and trim each corner to match the cardboard cover. Trim the back cover in the same way. There are two tricks to remember when trimming: do not attempt to trim the paper until the glue is bone-dry (wet paper will tear), and use a *new* razor blade. There is no need to line the inside of the covers unless you want to. If you do, apply the lining paper in exactly the same way.

If you want to cover a notebook that has *square* corners, start by pasting on paper as before, allowing ½ inch for the edges, and pressing the covered notebook overnight to allow the glue to dry. Then, turn the edges of the paper in, making a neat miter cut and fold at the corners, as shown in the illustration. Apply glue along the edges of the notebook and paste the paper down well inside it. Wipe away any extra glue with a slightly damp cloth or sponge. You will want to add lining paper to cover the turned-in edges, so measure, cut, and paste in the paper and press the book again. Plain construction paper that matches or complements one color of your printed pattern makes a very good lining.

*Making and Covering a Portfolio*

Ready-made portfolios can be bought in art stores and covered with printed papers in the same way as notebooks and memo pads. If the portfolio you buy has cord or ribbon ties, cut them off flush with a razor blade. You can also start from scratch and make a portfolio any size you want—smaller sizes are good for desk or letter portfolios. Whatever the size, a portfolio should be made of sturdy mat board, which you can buy at art stores and frame shops. Most shops will cut two pieces of board for you in whatever size you want. Mat board is a very stiff, nonwarping material (that's why it's good to use), and if you have to buy a large sheet and cut it yourself, the job must be done on a well-protected table with a thick-handled utility or mat knife. Stanley knives or the Miller's Falls brand are obtainable at hardware stores. You will also need a metal straightedge to guide your cuts, and a strong arm to do the job.

To make the portfolio, first cover the outsides of the two boards with your sheets of printed paper, centering the pattern on the boards. Leave one "raw" edge—here the edges of the paper and board should be even. This edge will be covered by the tape hinge. Leave ½ inch of extra paper around the other three edges. Press well under heavy books. Miter the corners (see the drawing on page 132) and turn the edges in and paste them down firmly on the insides of the boards. Wipe off any excess glue, put wax paper between the boards, and press them again under books.

To make the hinge, use 1½-inch plastic-*coated* cloth tape—

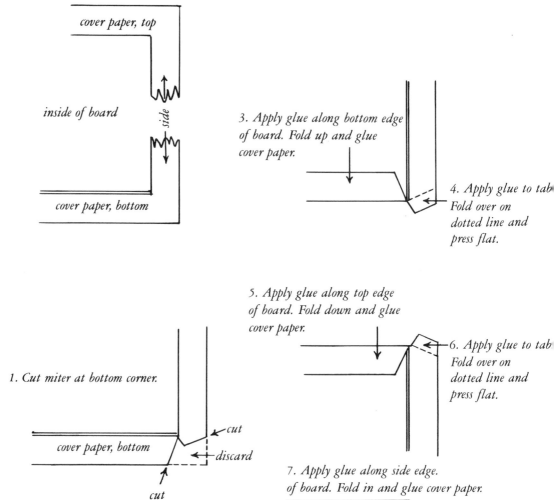

cover paper, top

inside of board

side

cover paper, bottom

3. Apply glue along bottom edge of board. Fold up and glue cover paper.

4. Apply glue to tab. Fold over on dotted line and press flat.

5. Apply glue along top edge of board. Fold down and glue cover paper.

6. Apply glue to tab. Fold over on dotted line and press flat.

1. Cut miter at bottom corner.

cover paper, bottom

cut

discard

cut

cover paper, top

cut

discard

cut

2. Cut miter at top corner.

7. Apply glue along side edge. of board. Fold in and glue cover paper.

glue

8. Glue in lining. Press.

*not* plastic tape (Mystik is a good brand)—in a color that goes well with your printed pattern. On the printed sides of the two covers draw a pencil line ¼ inch in from the "raw" edges of the covers to act as a guide for applying the hinge tape. Put one board on the very edge of the table, with the ruled line nearest you. Unroll and cut a length of tape that is 1 inch longer than your hinged edge. Leave an extra ½ inch of tape at each end and apply one long edge of the tape to the board, placing it along the drawn guideline. Do not allow the free edge of the tape to touch anything—it will stick! Turn the board over so that the sticky side of the tape is up.

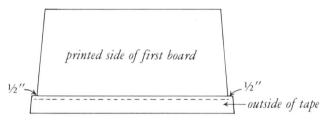

*printed side of first board*

½″ ½″

*outside of tape*

Now you must fasten a paper lining to the center part of the inside of the hinge, leaving ¼ inch of the edge of the tape free to be stuck to the other board. Cut a strip of any plain paper about 1 inch wide and the length of the cover. Stick this strip to the hinge, leaving the long ¼-inch edge and the ½-inch ends uncovered.

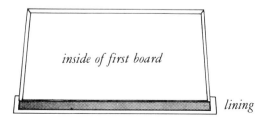

*inside of first board*

*lining*

Now place a ruler or yardstick on the table as shown and use it as a guide to line up the two boards. Place the second, untaped board printed side up, with the raw edge facing you, about a foot in from the edge of the table. Put the taped board on the table as shown, with the printed side up and the sticky edge of the tape down. Hold the tape up and out of the way and push the two boards close enough together so that you can apply the tape along the line you drew on the second, untaped board. Press the tape down well to join the two boards.

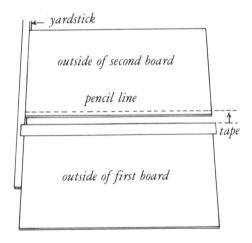

outside of second board

pencil line

outside of first board

Turn the portfolio over and fold the two ends of the hinge tape over the top and bottom of the covers. The hinge now needs to be lined inside with another, shorter length of cloth tape, to make a strong double hinge. Cut a piece of tape from the roll exactly the length of the hinge. Apply it, centered in the open space, and press it down in the center of the hinge first, holding the edges in your fingers as much as you can to keep the tape from sticking anywhere else but the center. Working from the center out, keep pressing the tape tightly along the edge of first one board, then the other, to make a little "step." Then press the tape down firmly on both boards. The little step will allow the hinge enough room to work well. If the long edges of the tape are not exactly even or straight along the boards, it does not matter—they will be covered by lining paper.

The measurements given here for attaching the hinge allow about 1 inch of space between the front and back covers, to accommodate the papers to be stored in the portfolio. If there is no need for that much space, just leave less room between the front and back boards when you apply the hinge. If you need *more* space, you cannot use Mystik tape, as it comes no wider than 1½ inches. You can, however, make a wider hinge out of cotton cloth, cut to fit, and stuck in place with white glue.

Now, unless you want to attach ties to the portfolio, all

there is left for you to do is to measure, mark off, and cut the two pieces of lining paper and paste them in.

If you want to attach ribbon or flat shoestring ties, do this just before you paste in the lining papers. Ties are not really necessary for a desk portfolio, but they are useful if a portfolio has to be carried around and small papers might slip out of it. Each tie should be about 10 inches long. Use a very sharp mat knife or razor blade and cut a slit the width of your ties in the center of each of the two covers, ½ inch from the edge opposite the hinge. Make the cuts from the outside of the covers. Push the cut end of each tie through the slits, from the outside to the inside of the covers, with a thin, dull blade.

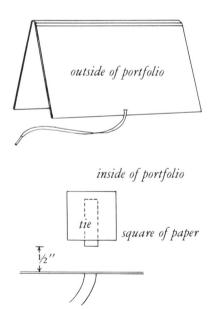

*outside of portfolio*

*inside of portfolio*

*tie*

*square of paper*

½″

Glue down 1 inch of the end of each tie and press it as flat as possible. Paste a 1-inch square of thin paper over it. If your portfolio is large, you can attach ties on all three open edges, centered and fastened in the same way.

Cut out and paste in the lining papers, press under heavy books while the glue dries, and your portfolio is finished.

*Designs for Covering Notebooks*

The illustrations below show some of the possibilities for using one little stamp—a smaller version of the practice stamp called the Rectangles in Chapter 2—to make three quite dif-

*actual size*

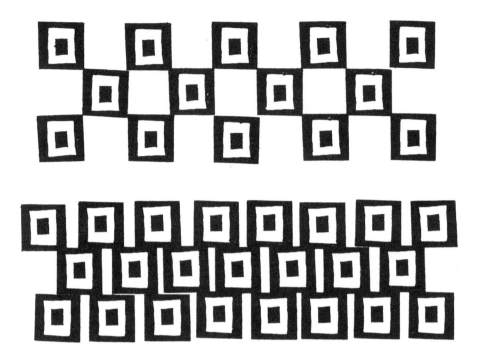

ferent repeat patterns. Notebook and portfolio covers are
good projects for printing patterns with simple geometric
designs—squares, circles, rectangles, and triangles. Keep in
mind that the size of your notebook should govern the scale
of your pattern—a very large unit does not look well repeated
on a tiny notebook, and a tiny pattern is not appropriate on
a large portfolio. Bright-colored paper printed in one or two
colors will produce some very handsome but unpretentious
designs.

# 12. PRINTING
# CLOTH BANNERS

A festive cloth banner bearing a printed personal message is a sort of glorified greeting card. Sometimes such banners are saved and hung up year after year on holiday occasions.

All four banners pictured here are printed with the hand-carved alphabet shown in Chapter 4; the small decorations will be familiar to you, too. The photographs show the basic design but not the color, and in a banner color is a very important element.

The Christmas banner is printed in black and green ink on stripes of red, white, green, and gold cotton material; the size is 6½ by 15¼ inches. The birthday banner is printed in blue and red on vertical panels of gold and aqua Indian Head cotton; the size is 4¾ by 16½ inches. The anniversary greeting is printed in red and blue on panels of gold and aqua cotton-Dacron broadcloth; the size is $7\frac{1}{2}$ by $6\frac{1}{2}$ inches. The valentine is printed in red on white hearts (made from iron-on material) that were pressed onto pink and red Indian Head cotton; the size is $7\frac{1}{2}$ by 14 inches.

Another kind of banner that is most welcome is a Get Well or Cheer Up banner made for a hospital patient who faces a long recovery.

### Selecting Cloth and Designing a Banner

A very good way to begin the printing of a banner on fabric is to buy a quarter yard each of several colors of finely woven all-cotton cloth or of cotton-and-Dacron broadcloth or shirting. The smoother and finer the cloth, the better it is for stamping. Select light to medium colors, and think of them in combination with each other. Bright, light colors will make a cheerful banner, and that's the way it ought to be.

In general, the best way to plan a banner is to design it on paper first, making a complete print of the message and decorations to act as your printing guide. Then cut out the cloth you need—adding an extra inch to the top and $\frac{1}{4}$ inch to each side—and press the material well. If you want to make a banner in more than one color, cut the fabric pieces to size,

allowing for a ¼-inch seam to sew the pieces together. Stitch by hand or machine in a thread that matches one of the pieces, and press the seams flat on the back.

*Printing on Cloth*

From each piece of cloth you have bought, cut a strip about 4 inches wide and 12 inches long. Working with alphabet letters and one carved decoration, try printing all your stamp-pad colors on each piece of cloth to find out which inks look best on what fabrics. Use plenty of ink and a firm pressure. These trial proofs will help you to decide on the colors for your banner.

The first thing you will discover is that stamp-pad inks do not print in full intensity on fabrics. This is because the inks are transparent and are absorbed by the threads of the cloth. Cloth soaks up ink far more than paper. So, in preparing to print, you should first ink the stamp pads very generously. As you print, add more ink to the pad as soon as a color loses a little of its intensity. After inking the stamp pad, always make trial proofs on scraps of cloth to be sure you won't get a blobby print.

You cannot make pencil guidelines for lettering on cloth, because the lines cannot be cleanly erased, but you can use a long, ½-inch-thick wooden guide stick. Put a piece of paper beneath your cloth and fasten it down with thumbtacks or transparent tape. Draw lines on the paper that extend beyond the edges of the fabric—to guide you in putting the stick in position.

Printing on fabric requires more ink and more pressure than printing on paper, but otherwise it presents no special problems. *A word of warning:* Stamp-pad inks are not colorfast, and printed fabrics should not be washed.

*Finishing a Printed Banner*

It is not absolutely necessary to line a banner by sewing on a backing piece, but a lining does give a more finished appearance. If you decide to line your banner, be sure that both pieces of cloth are exactly the same size, and that all the edges are cut very straight. Use a sewing machine if possible, or sew carefully by hand with small stitches. Attach the lining to the banner, with the right side of the lining facing the *right* or printed side of the banner. Stitch up one side, across the top, and down the other side as if you were making a pillowcase. Then turn the banner right side out, pull the seams out flat, and press. It is easier to sew in a very straight line if you first draw pencil guidelines.

If you do not want to put in a lining, you can simply leave the edges raw. This won't make much difference in the looks of the banner, and it means less work, of course. After the banner has been printed, if it seems to be pulled slightly out of shape, or if your margins are not quite of equal width, rule new edges, mark with a pencil, and cut the finished banner so it is square and true-sided.

The bottom edge, whether the banner is lined or not, should be cut to shape and left unhemmed—hemming would affect the way the cloth hangs. If there is a shaped or fancy end to be cut, design and draw it on heavy paper first, then cut out the paper pattern and draw around it on the cloth. Cut the marked end very carefully.

There are several ways to finish the top of a banner for hanging. For a small, lightweight banner, you can simply use a piece of cardboard as a stiffener for the top edge. Cut a strip of cardboard about $\frac{3}{8}$ inch wide and as long as the width of the finished banner. Put glue on both sides of the cardboard and fold the top of the banner around it. Add glue to the folded-over cloth and make another turn. Fold a piece of wax paper around the glued strip, and press under a heavy book. When the glue has dried, punch holes through both cardboard and cloth near the ends of the strip and attach a string hanger.

If your banner is lined, you can apply hanger loops made from cloth tape or from hemmed strips of the same cloth as the banner. Sew the two loops about $\frac{1}{2}$ inch from the corners of the lining, and put a small wooden dowel stick through the loops. The banner can be hung up on two pushpins or small nails, or by a string tied to the ends of the dowel.

You can also turn the top edge of the banner back— whether it is lined or not—and stitch a hem deep enough to hold a wooden dowel, with a string or thread tied to its ends for hanging. Remember to leave about 2 extra inches of cloth at the top if you decide to finish your work in this way.

If the banner must be wrapped as a gift, or if it must be mailed, roll it around a cardboard tube (from a roll of paper towels) with the printed side *out.* This will make the cloth hang better when it is unrolled. If you are going to mail a rolled banner, wrap it in several protective layers of heavy brown paper and tuck the ends of the paper into the ends of the tube.

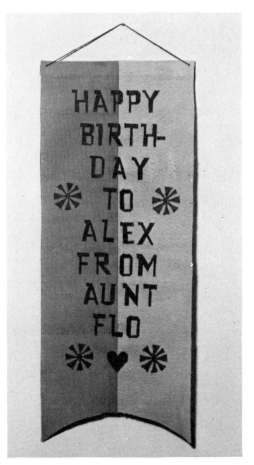

# SOURCES OF SUPPLY

ERASERS

*Artgum:* Faber-Castell and other similar brands

Art stores, stationery stores, school-supply stores

*White plastic:* Staedtler Mars. The "Grand" (large size), No. 526-52, cost about 80 cents each.

Art stores or by mail from:
Cloder Corporation
49-51 Ann Street
New York, NY 10038
*Minimum order:* Box of 10; about $8.00 plus postage

New York Central Supply Co.
62 Third Avenue
New York, NY 10003
*Minimum order:* $10.00

Bee-Ko Company, Inc.
155 East 44th Street
New York, NY 10017
*Minimum order:* Box of 10; about $8.00 plus postage

## KNIVES

X-Acto metal-handled, pencil-size knife with No. 16 blades

Art stores, hobby and modelmakers' shops, hardware stores

## RUBBER-STAMP ALPHABET PRINTING OUTFITS

*Office rubber-stamp printing outfits:* These are called Sign-Marker sets. Brands you can buy include Superior, Superb, Justrite, Atlas, Gripline, and Universal.

Office-supply stores, or ask your store if they will order a *Crown Marking Products Catalog* and price list from:

R. A. Stewart & Co., Inc.
85 White Street
New York, NY 10013

Or you can order such sets by mail from (write first for a price list):

Patrick & Co.
560 Market Street
San Francisco, CA
94104

*Toy printing sets*

Toy and hobby shops, or ask your local store if they will order sets from:

Superior Marking
   Equipment Co.
1800 West Larchmont
   Street
Chicago, IL 60613

Chemtoy Corp.
Cicero, IL 60650

Fleetwood Toy
   Corporation
1115 Broadway
New York, NY 10001

READY-MADE DECORATIONS, DESIGNS,
AND SILLY STUFF (individual stamps)

By mail from:

Bizzaro Rubber Stamps
P.O. Box 126
Annex Station
Providence, RI 02901
(Catalog $1.00)

Douglas Homs Corporation
1538 Industrial Way
Belmont, CA 94002
(Free catalog of "Dial-A
Phrase" stamps)

Squire & Small
178 Fifth Avenue
New York, NY 10010
(Free catalog)

STAMP PADS AND INKS

---

Carter's felt pads (not
sponge) and inks, or
Volger's Excelsior felt pads

Stationery stores,
office-supply stores

ACETATE PLASTIC SHEET

---

Use a notebook-sheet
protector or buy a sheet
of clear .03-point acetate

Art stores, office-supply
stores

GLUE

---

White glues (such as Elmer's,
Sobo, Ad-A-Grip) and
epoxy (Elmer's, Devcon
5-minute, etc.)

Hardware stores, variety
stores, drugstores,
school-supply stores

# Index

# ABOUT THE AUTHOR

Florence H. Pettit has had a lifelong interest in crafts and folk arts. Her first passion in art school was for hand printing of all kinds, and she still considers herself to be primarily a printer and fabric designer. This book, she says, was a "natural" for her. She is also a sculptor whose work has been shown in many museums and in three Smithsonian Institution exhibitions.

Mrs. Pettit has been a lecturer on historic American printed fabrics, and has served in various capacities with the Connecticut Commission on the Arts, the Southern Highlands Handicraft Guild, the American Crafts Council, and the Textile Department of the Cooper-Hewitt Museum of Design of the Smithsonian Institution. She is the author of seven books, including *How to Make Whirligigs and Whimmy Diddles and Other American Folkcraft Objects, Christmas All Around the House,* and *Mexican Folk Toys, Festival Decorations and Ritual Objects.*

Mrs. Pettit and her photographer husband, Robert, who has taken all the pictures for her books, live in Glenbrook, Connecticut.